TRUTH HELD HOSTAGE

AMERICA AND THE ARMENIAN GENOCIDE
– WHAT THEN? WHAT NOW?

John M. Evans

with a foreword by Dr. Dickran Kouymjian

For Der Torkom, *** Yeretsgin, and Gareen With 📖 my best, John Evans

Gomidas Institute
London

ISBN 978-1-909382-26-8

Gomidas Institute
42 Blythe Rd.
London W14 0HA
United Kingdom
www.gomidas.org
info@gomidas.org

For Donna and Jennifer

CONTENTS

Part II: The Armenian Genocide...

Part III: . . . And Us?

ILLUSTRATIONS

Foreword

by Dickran Kouymjian

Almost one century after Henry Morgenthau, the U.S. ambassador to the Ottoman Empire, shocked the world's conscience with his courageous and true account of the destruction of the Armenian people in their ancient homeland, another courageous and morally responsible former American ambassador has continued and updated the narrative with a personal and analytical memoir. Ambassador Morgenthau wrote about what happened to Armenians in the vast but decaying Ottoman Empire. He described an event that scholars and political leaders consider the first genocide of the twentieth century. Former ambassador John Evans writes as envoy to the Republic of Armenia, the latest iteration of an Armenian state born out of that genocidal destruction.

From the beginning, we are struck by the clarity of Ambassador John Evans's position, his honesty toward the historical record of the Armenian Genocide, and perhaps above all, his explicit faith in the democratic, humanitarian, and civically committed nature of his country, the United States. Ambassador Evans has faith in the American commitment to the principles of international justice and human rights the United States has always professed and almost always defended against opposing forces whether within or beyond its borders. He also expresses great faith in the Turks and their elected leaders in terms of their ability to reassess the history of the Ottoman Empire during the dark days of the Great War and to advance toward a just resolution of this unresolved catastrophe.

The book also describes the ambassador's unpredicted initiation to Armenia, its people, their history, and their hardships.

The well-constructed memoir of the truncated appointment of a career diplomat as ambassador to Armenia is about someone who ultimately refused to perpetuate an unconscionable policy. The policy imposed on him was based on the interests of certain forces and currents of thought within an inflexible contemporary U.S. State Department toward the concept of genocide, and the insistence, at almost any cost, on maintaining an indefensible attitude toward the distortions of history and toward an inculcated negationism by Turkey, a longstanding and militarily powerful NATO ally in the decades long Cold War and its aftermath. John Evans confesses at the beginning,

> In the course of learning about Armenia and its history, I encountered the highly controversial and painful historical issue that led me to question, and eventually break with, the policy of my own government, something I had never set out to do and did with no relish.

The success of the Turkish Government in its effort to influence American policy has a long history, going back to the activist work of Münir Ertegün, the first Turkish ambassador to the United States (1934–44). Trained as a legal expert, Ambassador Ertegün sided with Kemal Atatürk as early as 1920 and was the official legal counsel for Turkey during the negotiations at Lausanne, which overturned the early Treaty of Sèvres and left Armenia and the Armenians disenfranchised in the final peace settlement of World War I. Among Ambassador Ertegün's first decisive actions in favor of the Turkish denialist policy was his success in stopping Metro-Goldwyn-Mayer from completing and releasing a film on Franz Werfel's remarkable historic novel, *The Forty Days of Musa Dagh*. The 1933 novel, a compassionate retelling of the calculated elimination of Armenians from their historic lands, was banned by the Third Reich but published in English translation in 1934 and widely read. The ambassador's son Ahmet Ertegün, one of the founders of the famous Atlantic recording company that championed jazz, was subtler in his effort at countering continued sympathy for the large, post-Genocide Armenian population in America.

With the beginning of the Cold War, Turkey became an

important U.S. ally and the recipient of between two and four billion dollars a year. The country was absorbed as a member of NATO in 1952. American financing helped build the country's infrastructure, especially a system of roads in the former Armenian lands in the east of Asia Minor intended to allow the rapid deployment of the 30,000 American troops stationed in the country against a possible Soviet advance in the area. This financing, for more than half a century, represents an American investment of hundreds of billions of dollars. This important effort by the United States resulted in the creation of what is today a relatively rich country presenting a very important commercial space for a multitude of American industries, whether in the lucrative defense area or as a trading hub in the Middle East. The inordinate influence, if not control, of the American military-industrial complex on the State Department and with it, the Executive Branch's attitude and leniency toward the Turkish republic with regard to the question of the Armenian Genocide is widely acknowledged. Witness, for example, the rather mild rebuke recently to Turkey on the question of human rights, flagrantly abused at Gezi Park under the increasingly dictatorial Islamist regime of the former prime minister, now president, Recep Tayyip Erdoğan.

The lobbying efforts of Turkey are in part successful because, like other entities that can pressure the legislature and the diplomatic arm of our government—such as the tobacco lobby in former days, and those of big oil, lumber interests, and pharmaceuticals today—they have the clout or the money or both to pay for the best and most expensive K Street lobbying firms.

*

This personal history of an experienced Foreign Service officer, intertwined with that of the vagaries of American diplomacy, is extremely well documented. This is in no small part because John Evans has been fascinated by historical discourse ever since his days at Yale—one of the emblematic institutions of higher learning, whose graduates, including the younger President Bush, occupied and occupy so many important posts in the American government.

The narrative of events juxtaposes an extremely devoted civil servant with lucid ideas about how governments should conduct their affairs against what we now habitually call realpolitik. John Evans was and still is a genuinely loyal and fervent defender of this country, one whose primary concerns were both the proper interest of the nation and the well-being of, and justice for, humankind. He chronicles the conflict, both public and personal, between what he knew was right and what policy decided was necessary to protect certain perceived American interests. He tried to resolve the conflict by a sophisticated effort to nudge the policy of the State Department, of which he was part, toward an honest expression of what happened to the Armenians during the years 1915–23 and the idea of embracing the concept of genocide against violent cynicism and uncompromising distortion.

John Evans was not a whistle blower.

Or perhaps it is better to say that he worked with a moral commitment to bring his superiors to look carefully at policy and harmonize what had been said on the Armenian Genocide by the White House with the more conservative, traditional views of State. In April 2005 he was chosen to receive the Christian A. Herter Award for Constructive Dissent by a Senior Officer. It was for his earnest efforts to bring more reflection and simply correct history into policy decisions on Armenian-Turkish relations and the general question of genocide that he was chosen for the honor, given annually to a Foreign Service Officer who was willing to express unpopular positions. Evans's nomination for the Herter award was announced in a world-wide telegram signed by Condoleezza Rice but was rescinded on a technicality and no Herter Award was conferred that year.

Throughout the book, Ambassador Evans's writing is never self-justification. Rather, it is an exercise in presenting things as they were and still are. He worked with his superiors, and even after having been let down, perhaps even betrayed, by them, instead of cutting ties, continued to maintain correct, even cordial relations. After all, they had worked, and in some cases had studied, together for decades. The events occurred well before the Snowden affair, with which it shares only the same desire to make official American policy more transparent and more firmly grounded on historical fact and ethical principles.

Near the end of his narrative, the ambassador turns to a prescriptive phase, trying to present a personal reply to the perpetual question: "What is to be done?"

Ambassador Evans offers ten modest proposals. This is not the place to review them one by one or to even list them. Readers will discover and reflect on them individually. But one proposal, the third, offers an opportunity for further elaboration: "The President of the United States, in the tradition of both Woodrow Wilson and Ronald Reagan should recognize the Armenian Genocide as an historical fact."

In President Wilson's time speaking of the Armenian Genocide was significantly more than just recognition of a crime against humanity. It was a mobilization—an unprecedented mobilization—of the entire population of America to help another distant people, a nation of orphans. In early September 1915, at the start of the deliberate Young Turk policy of eliminating or reducing to insignificance non-Turkish, non-Muslim minorities of the Ottoman Empire, which constituted one-quarter to one-third of the population of Turkey during the war, Ambassador Morgenthau wrote to the State Department the fateful words, "Destruction of the Armenian race in Turkey is progressing rapidly." He urged his superiors to contact a number of notables, including Cleveland Dodge, to bring together philanthropically minded individuals as well as industrial and political figures, to help stop the massacres and forced exile and to prepare to give aid to those Armenians who survived. This action led to Near East Relief organizing the first important charitable campaign in America's history, one directed toward Armenian survivors, especially orphans. The goal was to raise 30 million dollars, an unbelievable sum at the beginning of the twentieth century. More dramatic was that well over a 100 million dollars were collected, with donations from every school and college in the country, every city and county, and all of the states. The call for contributions and aid extended beyond the end of the war, with appeals not just from President Wilson, but after, by both President Warren Harding and President Calvin Coolidge. Equally remarkable, and a further sign of how much the plight of the Armenians impregnated the very fiber of the country, all three wives of three successive presidents adopted at least one Armenian child. None of this aid could have been successfully distributed without the Near East Relief, of course, but also without the cooperation of the U.S. State Department—the same State Department that is today so susceptible to lobbying and other pressures rather than the moral certitude that dominated the mindset of diplomats of that time.

John Evans is a direct inheritor of this unambiguous tradition of compassion and succor for a clearly persecuted people who were subjected to one of the first deliberate extinctions of a nation in modern times.

Ambassador Evans follows in the tradition of Woodrow Wilson in the sense that his own modus operandi was one of dignified diplomacy. He always insisted on the importance of what can certainly be called a highly ethical attitude toward governing and interacting with all peoples. In gratitude to the unprecedented outpouring of charity on the part of American citizens led by three successive presidents, the very orphans that were helped wove an immense rug (nearly 12 x 19 feet) in the Near East Relief orphanage for Armenians in Ghazir, Lebanon. Made of nearly four and a half million knots and executed by seven of the orphan girls in ten months, it was dedicated and sent to President Coolidge, who received it at the White House on December 4, 1925. The famous orphan rug has been in storage in recent years; the Smithsonian Institution announced it would be shown at an event on December

16, 2013, which included a book launch on the weaving of the orphan rug, but canceled the display after the White House refused to loan the carpet, probably under protest from Turkey or those under its influence. The Orphan Rug was finally put on display for a couple of weeks at the While House Visitor's center on November 18, 2014. Ambassador Evans was among those at the opening, expressing the same dissatisfaction with the approach of President Barack Obama's administration as he had with that of President George W. Bush. He was quoted as referring to the concession to finally allow the showing or display of the beautiful carpet with its very symbolic meaning thus: "It's a very miserly recognition."

The book *Truth Held Hostage* will be an eye opener for many, perhaps mostly for Armenian Americans who are often naïve about how their government works or who refuse to give up their total loyalty to the United States and the historical rationale on which it was founded and is still nurtured. The behind-the-scenes workings of the State Department, including decision-making and control of policy, will no doubt disillusion many who imagine that the democratic process as practiced in America should obviate such behavior; it will also reinforce the opinion of a small minority that the struggle for true justice is even tougher than imagined.

But Ambassador Evans throughout this extremely well-crafted book always tries to keep the discussion moving toward solutions to the very problems he has struggled with, namely the recognition and acceptance of the crime against humanity perpetrated against the Armenians by a Young Turk government, while promoting reconciliations between Turks and Armenians—the Republics of Armenia and Turkey—with the active engagement of the United States. These threads are carefully woven together in his ten proposals, which he calls modest, toward such a mutual understanding and acceptance. In his final, "Thinking Ahead" section, he contextualizes the Armenian Genocide, around the time of its centennial, through a series of analogous conflicts faced by the United States and other nations.

The book is in many respects a twenty-first century sequel to Ambassador Morgenthau's wake-up call, one just as carefully written, in an admirable and very readable style, interested as much in the important principles it espouses as its explanation of what happened to Ambassador Evans because he chose consciously to use the taboo expression "Armenian Genocide" while exercising his function as representative of the United States government.

On a personal note, I lived many of the seminal moments in his work in Yerevan. I was one of the scholars invited to the 90th Genocide anniversary conference organized in Yerevan in 2005, and the chair of one of the sessions. I remember very clearly the presence of Donna Evans, the ambassador's wife, in the front rows, and the absence of the ambassador, who was not allowed to attend. My wife and I also came to join Hrant Dink, Taner Akçam, and Murat Belge on the outside terrace of the Armenia Hotel after the last session, a moment after a glass of wine was thrown at Murat by a disgruntled young extremist. Even before the dinner the next evening, which Ambassador Evans describes in his memoir, where he met Dink, Akçam, and Belge, the latter immediately dismissed the young man's gesture with a laugh, saying that he had confronted many worse abuses regularly from his own countrymen in Turkey. This was a theme already brought up by Baskın Oran, one of the Turkish speakers at the conference, when asked a question from the audience after his paper.

I was also at Fresno State University, as director of the Armenian Program, when the ambassador openly used the term Armenian Genocide.

John Evans having done his homework on the historical, legal and ethical issues is remarkably solid in his analysis of the past century. He firmly insists on the value to the United States, to Armenia and to humankind, of holding up such ideals. To many, these ideals may appear unattainable. But the message Ambassador Evans is trying to pass on is that change is possible: change for the better. One should never stop trying even when confronted by roadblocks that seem impassable.

As an American I can only applaud the clarity and professionalism with which Ambassador Evans has been able to uphold the historical dignity of our country while openly, but without malice, criticizing one of its untenable, almost inexplicable errors of judgment. John Evans explains it all so well that any derivative attempt to retell what he has written so clearly and convincingly in this book would be redundant.

Ambassador Evans constantly appeals to his fellow citizens to look carefully at the actions their elected representatives are taking, voluntarily or under pressure, on matters of genocide and human rights everywhere. He wants them to focus not just on those countries that for the moment our foreign policy deems to be unfriendly toward the United States. In the final analysis it is not just the State Department that has a lot to learn from the mature analysis of John Evans, and not just the Turkish governing elite, but also the Armenians, whether in the Republic of Armenia or in America and other countries. He provides the background to Armenian anger and indignation toward American policy, but also for the understanding of Turkish denial and the rewriting of its own history. Fortunately in that effort more and more young Turkish scholars, intellectuals, and human rights advocates are joining him.

Dickran Kouymjian

The author is Haig & Isabel Berberian Endowed Professor of Armenian Studies (Emeritus), California State University, Fresno, and a member of the Armenian Academic of Sciences, Yerevan and the Accademia Ambrosiana, Milan.

Preface

A few years ago, while serving as the U.S. ambassador to Armenia, I collided head-on with one of the biggest taboos in American foreign policy: the issue of the 1915 Armenian Genocide in Ottoman Turkey.

While the vast majority of historians and experts on genocide years earlier had concluded that the events of 1915-16 constituted the "first genocide of the twentieth century" – that is, the first modern case of genocide – the Republic of Turkey vehemently denied it, and the U.S. Government supported Turkey in its version of those far-off events, for reasons of current foreign policy, especially the Iraq War, and out of habitual deference to the concerns of its long-standing ally.

Although I had no Armenian family, business or other connections of any sort, I nonetheless found myself challenged to make an agonizing choice between the historical truth of the matter – that the Armenians had been the object of a genocidal campaign instigated by the Young Turks – and the official "line," that there may have been an "annihilation," "forced deportations" or even "murder," but that the term "genocide" somehow did not fit the case. The subject was, in fact, strictly taboo at the State Department and everywhere else in the U.S. Government.

This book tells the story of how I dealt with this personal and professional dilemma, an issue of conscience unlike any I had ever previously encountered. For better or for worse, I concluded that the question of the Armenian Genocide simply had to be addressed, whatever the personal consequences for me and my career. Alas, it remains firmly on the international agenda, because Armenians and Turks are still trapped in this tragic and complex issue. But the issue is not static. Courageous Turkish intellectuals have been gradually laboring away to make progress toward a more truthful accounting for what was done. New materials have been unearthed. Armenian and Turkish scholars and public figures have made important breakthroughs in understanding the past and attempting to deal with its consequences. With the 100th anniversary of the Genocide in 2015 now receding, it seems an appropriate moment for me to put forward my own modest contribution. Besides telling my own story, I hope to suggest some ways to move the issue forward with everyone's honor and dignity – and the truth – intact.

Some readers may be curious about my personal story; many people have encouraged me to tell it. Others may be interested in the legal, historical and geopolitical aspects of the issue and its current relevance to the stability and security of the Caucasus Region in our day. I have tried, therefore, to write this book for both groups, recounting my own intellectual journey, then moving to discuss the moral and policy issues. Whether this approach succeeds, the reader will have to judge for himself.

A number of people read early drafts of my manuscript, among them the poet, memoirist and scholar Peter Balakian, former Ambassador Ed Djerejian, the writer George Held, the Honorable Paul Ignatius, Edith Khachaturian, former Foreign Service colleagues including Wayne Merry, Henry Precht and the late Nelson Ledsky, Canadian lawyer Harry Dikranian, Stan Norris of the Natural Resources Defense Council, Alex van Oss of the Foreign Service Institute, Charly Ghailian of the USC Institute of Armenian Studies, and Vartkes Yeghiayan of the Center for Armenian Remembrance. All of them encouraged me at critical moments in the process of researching and writing this book, and Alice Nighoghosian advised me on publishing. A few have criticized me for not giving equal time to the official Turkish position. To them I would say that my stand is not just "pro-Armenian"; it is "pro-Truth," and, in the long run, therefore, also "pro-Turkish." Any errors of fact and judgment are, of course, ultimately my own. I stress in addition that, although the U.S. Department of State has reviewed my manuscript for any disclosure of classified information (which would have been inadvertent on my part), the opinions and characterizations in this book are mine alone, and do not represent official positions of the U.S. Government.

Introduction

As a nation, we Americans instinctively prefer to look to the future, not the past, to "let bygones be bygones," and, when something painful has befallen a friend, to advise: "just get over it." As George Will once pointed out, when Americans say "it's history," we mean *it no longer matters*: something like saying "it's toast." This puts us in a minority among the world's peoples, a happy minority in which we are joined by the Australians and possibly two thirds of the Canadians. This future orientation of ours may at times have served us well as a basis for our national strength and optimism, but it complicates our deeper understanding of the world beyond our shores. How can we be expected to understand the Serbs, who still nurse the wounds of having been defeated in 1389 by the Ottomans at Kosovo Polje, a defeat that Serbian nationalists have portrayed as the crucible of the Serbian nation and the basis for their continuing claim to Kosovo? Or the Shiites, who march in the streets and flagellate themselves in penitence on Ashura, the grim holiday marking the martyrdom of Hussein, grandson of the Prophet? There are other examples that could be cited from nearly every part of the globe.

Because we are not aware of history, we often don't "get it." We "don't get it" that one of the world's oldest nations – the Armenians – came close to being annihilated less than one hundred years ago in the first major instance of genocide of the 20th Century.[*] Some of us have been telling the now far-flung descendants of those who survived either that "it wasn't really genocide," that they "brought it on themselves," or that they should "just get over it." Sadly enough,

---

[*] Some genocide scholars consider the 1904-06 annihilation of the Hereros in German South West Africa to have been the first instance of genocide in the twentieth century. See, for example, Jon Bridgman and Leslie Worley in Chapter 1 of *Century of Genocide* (New York: Routledge, 2004, Samuel Totten, William Parsons and Israel Charny, editors).

this approach, as I found out, is partly the product of an official policy of denial by the Turkish State, but also of the continuing acquiescence in that denial by our own government, with the prominent exception of former President Ronald Reagan, who knew from his California experience that there had been a genocide, but whose advisors persuaded him to stop saying so after he boldly used the term in 1981.[*]

An unpredictable set of circumstances taught me something about the Armenians during my professional career in the U.S. Foreign Service. Through no particular design on anyone's part, I came to be named U.S. Ambassador to the small, land-locked country that is now the Republic of Armenia. Hard to find on the map, this new, post-Soviet state is located south of Russia, in the Southern Caucasus Mountains, nestled between Turkey, Georgia, Azerbaijan and Iran. In the course of learning about Armenia and its history, I encountered the highly controversial and painful historical issue that led me to question, and eventually break with, the policy of my own government, something I had never set out to do and did with no relish.

The fact of the matter is that the Armenians of Anatolia (present-day Turkey) were nearly annihilated in 1915-16 in an effort by Turkish nationalists, led by a faction of the Young Turks, to create an "Anatolia for the Turks" under the cover of World War I, as the decrepit multinational Ottoman Empire was tottering toward its collapse. I started out knowing next to nothing about those events, but eventually came to a point where my conscience demanded I make a choice and take a stand on this issue. Having done so while serving as an American Ambassador, I probably owe the public an explanation. I will recount one personal adventure from Iran at the time of the Shah because it shows both Turkic Azeris and Armenians in a shared environment where I first got to know them. But I will also venture some suggestions as to what might reasonably be done to

---

[*] Ronald Reagan, Presidential Proclamation 4838 dated April 22, 1981.

help Armenians and Turks overcome the bitter relations that now exist between them, in part because of their unresolved differences over the historical issue of 1915. Not everyone will approve or applaud my suggestions. Some may find them too radical, others, not radical enough. They are suggestions, and nothing more. Because of our position in world affairs, we Americans have an important role to play in helping the Armenians and the Turks reconcile their differences. Avoiding, or denying, the truth about what happened in 1915-16 is not only unethical; in the long run it is untenable.

Many American readers are already vaguely aware of the Armenian Genocide, but are puzzled, put off, or maybe even annoyed by the competing claims of Armenian-Americans – the Armenian *diaspora* – and the Government of Turkey. For most of us, on seeing a demonstration in Washington, New York or on a college campus, our natural American reaction is to turn a deaf ear to both sides. Not only are we Americans not very interested in history, we also don't much care for "unnecessary" controversy of the sort that filled the American media in October 2007 when a Congressional committee was considering a resolution entitled "Affirming the United States Record on the Armenian Genocide." But the very intensity of the debate that this issue always generates should be a clear signal that something deadly serious is at stake. The Armenian Genocide is not simply a historical question from a far-away time and place of no relevance to us. In particular, the continuing presence of genocide in our world, most notably today in parts of Africa, reminds us that our attitude toward past genocides shapes the climate in which modern-day atrocities can take place. We Americans need to look into it and see what this is all about, starting with what has been called the "forgotten genocide."

Although this book does not attempt original historical research in the Ottoman or Armenian archives, it contains some comments on the basic literature that should be useful to those who are new to the topic, as well as some personal observations.

A Special Note to Armenian Readers...

Armenians in the Republic of Armenia and in the Diaspora, whose opinions about the Genocide and especially about how it should be approached vary greatly, have shared their views with me in many private and public settings, and I have tried at least to take those views into account in preparing this book. When I have spoken to Armenian groups, I have often felt that we were speaking to each other in isolation from the national and international mainstream. It is obviously easier and more comfortable to have a private conversation than a public one; however, the Armenian Genocide needs to be understood and discussed not only by Armenians and Turks, but by our fellow citizens whose names might be Smith, Jones or O'Reilly. My book is an attempt to broaden a conversation that has too long been conducted in church halls and Armenian community gatherings from which "odars" ("others") like me were absent. I am not Armenian, although I greatly sympathize with the historical plight of your people. My book is written in part for you. It is written especially for those Armenian-Americans who heard me use the forbidden word "genocide" at UCLA, in Fresno and at UC Berkeley in February, 2005, when I was traveling as the U.S. Ambassador to Armenia, and could not fathom why I was consequently removed from my post by the U.S. State Department. I have received a number of piecemeal inquiries about why I said what I said; this book will attempt to answer those questions for the record.

My book is also in part for those hardy Americans and others of Armenian descent living and working in Yerevan, in today's Republic of Armenia, who looked on in amazement as I was forced to apologize for my public statements about the Genocide, received – and was then denied – the Christian A. Herter Award of the American Foreign Service Association for "constructive dissent by a senior officer," and departed my post one year early on orders from Washington, all while successfully carrying out U.S. policy in other areas. These Armenian-Americans, today "repatriated" to Armenia, supported me in 2006 by organizing a "yellow ribbon campaign" that drew thousands of supporters from among Armenians of all ages and categories on Armenian Remembrance Day, April 24.

...And to Turkish, Azeri and Jewish Readers

I hope this book will also interest patriotic Turks and Turkish-Americans who are vaguely uneasy about the facts of what happened in 1915 in the late Ottoman Empire, but are particularly concerned about the possible consequences, both for themselves and for their homeland, of the Genocide's being recognized officially by the United States Congress, as it came very close to doing in the fall of 2007 and may do under a future U.S. Administration. I invite these readers to risk thinking this issue through with a former American diplomat who bears Turks and Turkey no ill will, has worked closely with many Turkish colleagues over the years, was attracted to the study of Ottoman history, and thinks of Istanbul as one of the greatest cities of the world. I invite Azeri readers also to think through these questions with me, keeping in mind their many interactions – some positive, some negative – with Armenians in the Soviet Union and putting aside for a moment the high emotions that attach to the as-yet-unresolved standoff over Nagorno-Karabakh. I hope also that Jewish readers, naturally solicitous of the interests of the State of Israel, which has traditionally been militarily and diplomatically close to Ankara, may find this book helpful in their own deliberations about the ethical dilemma the Armenian Genocide poses with particular poignancy for them.

Whether I was right or wrong to engage publicly on this issue while serving as U.S. Ambassador to Armenia, my main intention today is to suggest some ways forward that might help Armenians and Turks alike to come to terms with the historical truth but also gradually to reconcile their differences and build a better future for all the people who inhabit Anatolia and the Caucasus, regardless of nationality. I also suggest some ways in which the United States might attempt to deal with the unresolved issue of the Armenian Genocide, the 100th anniversary of which, in 2015, is now behind us.

This book is in three parts: in Part One I recount my own intellectual journey from knowing next to nothing about the Armenians, the Ottoman Empire, or genocide, to comprehending at least some basic truths about all three; in Part Two I examine the legal and political context that today surrounds the issue of the Genocide; and in Part Three I advance some suggestions as to what might be done on all sides to deal with this sensitive and painful question.

TRUTH
HELD
HOSTAGE

AMERICA AND THE ARMENIAN GENOCIDE
– WHAT THEN? WHAT NOW?

Part I
Voyage of Discovery

Starting in the Dark

As our aircraft hurtled through the darkness of eastern Turkey's airspace, my wife Donna and I began to wonder how far away Armenia really could be. We were used to relatively short hops from Western Europe to Prague and St. Petersburg, our most recent Foreign Service postings, but this was unprecedented. The flight just went on and on. And below, hardly any lights: nothing like the gleaming agglomerations of London, Brussels, Paris or Frankfurt. Finally, at midnight or so, we saw some flickers of light, widely separated, on the uneven ground below. Our British Air pilots began the descent. We exchanged glances, donned our American flag lapel pins and held hands as the aircraft precipitately lurched downwards. At last: a hard landing and a rush of torrid air; it was the hot August of 2004. Uniformed guards took our passports and whisked us away in a special van to the VIP Lounge of Yerevan's Zvartnots Airport. Although I had discouraged it, on account of the late hour, the senior staff of the U.S. Embassy had gathered at the airport, according to Foreign Service tradition, to welcome their new ambassador. They were lined up in protocol order, starting with Anthony Godfrey, my future deputy, who had, by mutual agreement, preceded me to Yerevan by three weeks. As I greeted each new colleague in turn, I gained the sense that this was a solid, serious team of U.S. Foreign Service officers. For their part, these men and women seemed relieved to see for themselves that the new ambassador and his spouse were approachable human beings, if a bit the worse for wear. What neither they nor we imagined on that auspicious night was how eventful our two years in Armenia were to be, not only because of day-to-day challenges, but thanks to still-unburied ghosts and unexpected, unbidden voices of conscience.

Having briefly met our new colleagues, Donna and I collapsed into an armored limousine (an old and creaky but still serviceable lightly-armored Ford), and headed for the Armenian capital city of

Yerevan with Haik Poghosian, our Armenian driver, at the wheel and my new deputy, Anthony Godfrey, in the front seat. For me, Haik, a short, sturdy, good-looking fellow with a ready smile and one gold tooth, brought back a memory from thirty years earlier, from my first assignment in Tehran, where the Ambassador's driver was an Armenian with an almost identical name: Haikaz. According to national mythology, the progenitor of the Armenian people was Haik, who fought off Babylonian foes and led his clan to the Armenian Highland, which Armenians subsequently called "Hayastan." On the way into town, in the pitch black of night, we suddenly found ourselves surrounded by garish casinos, the local equivalent of Las Vegas, complete with flashing neon lights, lining both sides of the road. This was the first surprise of many that awaited us in Armenia. Anthony Godfrey explained that the casinos had been forced out of the capital, where they were not appreciated by the citizenry, and relocated right at the city's border in next-door Armavir province. Certainly the scene typified the "Wild East" atmosphere we had come to know in Russia and other parts of the former Soviet Union. Eventually we reached the center of Yerevan. A beautifully lit church on the bluffs overlooking the Hrazdan River gave hints, through the darkness, of architectural excellence and cultural depths to be explored. As we proceeded up the main street, Mashtots Avenue, we noticed that Yerevan, though geographically of the Middle East, had a distinctly European look to it. Even at that late hour, cafés bustled, people strolled along arm-in-arm, and all was brightly lit. Turning into the alley that led to our official residence, we could see, even in the dim light, that it was a relatively ramshackle affair. No matter. We knew Yerevan was what the State Department called a "hardship" assignment, and that four ambassadorial couples had inhabited this rented house before us. Despite the late hour, our Armenian domestic staff, Ovsanna, Anahit, and Marat, were on hand to greet us, shy and a bit nervous on meeting their new employers. They had put flowers everywhere and cleaned the house spotless. Anthony took his leave, as did the house staff, and Donna and I, exhausted, gave thanks that we had finally made it to our first ambassadorial post, with all the initial indicators pointing positive. It had been a wonderful welcome, and by this time it was early on a Saturday morning, so we turned in for some much-needed rest.

The next day dawned with brilliant sunshine. Still groggy, we were taken to the architecturally imposing Republic Square for lunch at the public nerve center of diplomatic life, the terrace café of the Marriott Armenia Hotel. The hotel is located just steps from the Foreign Ministry, and its sidewalk café is Yerevan's equivalent of the Café de la Paix, where, if you sit long enough, everyone in the world eventually shows up. Within minutes of arriving at the café, we had been introduced to Thorda Abbott-Watt, the British Ambassador, and several other significant personalities, so intimate and informal is life in that small capital. After a day of casual sightseeing, back at our official residence, we discovered what was to become our favorite spot, especially at night: the balcony that surrounded the house on the upper level, like a box seat in the theater of the city's lights and sounds – including the songs of lovelorn cats at night and the cawing of peacocks by day. On one of our first evenings, with the sultry summer weather still oppressing, we listened with a mixture of horror and amusement as one of these crooning felines (a real "cat on a hot tin roof") slipped and clawed its way down a nearby roof and fell off with an audible thud to the alley below. In the distance blinked the omnipresent Yerevan television tower – the local version of *La Tour Eiffel* – and the far-off lights of Nork Marash, a hilly section of town with many new, chic houses and views of Mt. Ararat, the imposing volcanic peak that dominates the Armenian capital from the other side of the Turkish-Armenian border, near and yet impossibly far.

The Republic of Armenia is not big – only about the size of Maryland, with a smaller population. On that very first Sunday, Haik, our driver, took us on his version of a Cook's Tour that lasted all of one very long summer's day. We started by visiting the Cathedral at Etchmiadzin, the seat of the Catholicos of the Armenian Apostolic Church: the approximate Armenian equivalent of the Vatican. Arriving just as Sunday High Mass was ending, we witnessed the solemn spectacle of priests and the devout moving through those ancient precincts. Next Haik took us to see the massive statue of his namesake Haik, the founder of the Armenian nation. It was his choice to do so and we humored him. Then we were off to the Hellenistic temple at Garni, an imposing edifice dating to ancient times (destroyed in 1679 by an earthquake but reconstructed). Next, Haik took us to the church and monastery complex at Geghard, carved into living rock. Finally, as if to prove that, with a good driver, one could see all of Armenia in a single day, Haik drove us into the mountains past alpine Lake Sevan and through a twisting wooded valley to the monastery at Haghartsin, an airy but now deserted church compound overlooking the valley below that speaks powerfully of the country's past glories. On the way we stopped to dine on fish – the famous and succulent lake trout known as *ishkhan* – at a restaurant on the Sevan Peninsula. An island before Soviet-era irrigation projects lowered the water level of the lake by some fifteen meters, the peninsula was home to both a monastery and the summer residence of Armenia's President, Robert Kocharian. Lake Sevan, still unspoiled by motorboats, was, and is, a magnificent feature of Armenia.

Though it left us exhausted, this first trip around our new country of assignment constituted one of the happiest days of our entire stay in Armenia. I had not yet presented my diplomatic credentials – the diplomatic equivalent of "coming out" – and no one recognized me. I now understand this was an advantage. Later, after I had publicly uttered the word "genocide," I became such an inadvertent hero to the Armenian people that it was almost embarrassing to appear in public: everyone by then knew me by sight, knew what I had done, and wanted to have photos snapped with me. It was a form of celebrity I had not wanted or ever sought, and it went against my diplomatic instinct, which had always been to avoid controversy and remain discreetly out of the public eye. During our whole time in Armenia, both Donna and I went about the country without bodyguards, something neither of my colleagues, the U.S.

ambassadors in neighboring Georgia and Azerbaijan, could afford to do, despite the good relations the United States happily enjoyed with those nations. At more than ninety percent ethnic Armenian, and at least nominally Christian, the Republic of Armenia is one of the few truly pro-American and pro-Western countries in the region. There is no undercurrent of Islamic fundamentalism, as in Azerbaijan, or sympathy for the Chechen rebels, as in Georgia. Although it is Indo-European, the distinct and difficult Armenian language makes outsiders immediately stand out. Russian is still widely spoken there, as elsewhere in the former Soviet Union, but English is heard more and more, especially among younger people. Later in my tour of duty, there was another reason we felt entirely secure in Armenia: after I had become well-known for my statements about the Genocide, I felt that all Armenians were keeping an eye out for me and my wife. We continued to walk about freely in Yerevan on the weekends, attended concerts and even shopped in the open-air markets, never experiencing a hostile glance or action – except once, from an Iranian student.[*]

One of the many substantive reasons the United States and its ambassador were so popular in Armenia was the U.S. Peace Corps and its programs in public health, English-teaching, business education and the environment. In contrast to some other countries – Russia, for example – Armenia welcomed the Peace Corps. My first official act, even before presenting credentials, was to swear in the twelfth class of Peace Corps trainees; in fact, we had accelerated our arrival in Yerevan in order that I might do so. The Peace Corps volunteers came in all sizes and ages, and we valued them highly for their dedication, plucky attitude toward the privations they faced in isolated villages, and spirit of service. We got to know a number of

---

* Donna once saw a young man on the street make an obscene gesture as our car, with the flag flying, passed by. We later positively identified the man as an Iranian student when he was interviewed on Armenian television during the Iranian Presidential elections that brought Ahmadinejad to power.

the volunteers personally and made a point of looking them up when we visited the villages where they worked. Truly, "one of the best faces America has ever projected is the face of a Peace Corps volunteer."[*]

Remember the Starving Armenians!

I grew up in Williamsburg, Virginia, a mile from Jamestown, the first permanent English settlement in the New World, where nearly all the other children bore Anglo-Saxon surnames and attended (mostly) Protestant churches on Sunday. In those days, in the 1950s, I was totally unaware that such a people as "the Armenians" even existed. To be sure, my grandmother habitually admonished us, as we sat down to dinner during holiday visits to Penn Cottage, her house in the staid Philadelphia suburb of Wynnewood, to "remember the starving Armenians!" We duly cleaned our plates, and that was that: Grandma had accomplished her purpose and we gave the "starving Armenians" no further thought.

My grandparents on both sides were of a generation of Americans that read the New York *Times* and the Philadelphia *Inquirer;* they surely knew about the atrocities of 1915, but never spoke about them to us grandchildren. Other Americans have told me they also heard that phrase, "remember the starving Armenians," but didn't connect it with anything they could relate to. Some Armenians today find the admonition offensive. They should not. The American response to the Armenian crisis was, in the words of Hovig Tchalian, "the first international human rights movement in American history and helped define the nation's emerging global identity."[†] But Americans today are largely unaware of their grandparents' – or great-

---

[*] Teresa Heinz Kerry at the 2004 Democratic National Convention.

[†] Hovig Tchalian, "Genocide and the historical imagination," Critics' Forum, in *Armenian Reporter* Arts and Culture, April 5, 2008, pp C10-11. Americans contributed some $117m to Near East Relief.

grandparents' – involvement, save for the "starving Armenians" phrase (which may have been first used by Clara Barton).

That such prominent Americans as Woodrow Wilson and Theodore Roosevelt were, in their time, vocal and active in support of the Armenians is now largely forgotten, although Peter Balakian's 2003 book *The Burning Tigris* retrieved and presented some of that history to modern American readers.*

It is not only Americans who are largely unaware of the Armenian Genocide. Donald Bloxham has written, "...the Armenian genocide has yet to enter the collective consciousness of most non-Armenians."†

My father taught English Literature at the College of William and Mary in Virginia, specializing in the English Renaissance. His time and cultural horizons encompassed ancient civilizations and philosophies and the Classical and Biblical lands. Dad read Greek and Latin easily, and one of my best memories is of working with him to translate fragments of Plautus and Terence. Not religious, he taught a course on the Bible "as literature." One might have expected otherwise in an academic household, but the Armenians simply were not a presence in my early life. My mother had studied art at the Pennsylvania Academy of the Fine Arts, and had had a successful painting career before marriage to my father and my family's move from Philadelphia to Williamsburg. Socially, my parents knew no Armenians. When, in 1963, I went away to St. Andrew's School in Delaware, to obtain more Latin, more history and more sports than were then available in the Williamsburg public schools, I still managed to maintain my near-total ignorance about the Armenians. In my time at St. Andrew's, there was only one Catholic boy and one Jew; the rest of us were Protestants, mostly Episcopalians, as was the

---

* Peter Balakian, *The Burning Tigris: The Armenian Genocide and America's Response*. New York: HarperCollins, 2003.

† Donald Bloxham, *The Great Game of Genocide: Imperialism, Nationalism and the Destruction of the Ottoman Armenians*. New York: Oxford University Press, 2005, p. 6.

school itself. The atmosphere there was not nearly so rigidly traditional as portrayed in the Robin Williams movie *The Dead Poets Society*, filmed on the St. Andrew's campus. Still, it reflected those times: all boys, coats and ties for all classes, study halls, chapel nearly every day, a class in "Sacred Studies," and a rigorous schedule of required sports. Out of curiosity, I recently checked with my old school's Alumni Office and learned that there was an Armenian-American in the Class of 1949, and have been quite a few since then. This actually makes sense once one knows that when the first small groups of Armenians reached America in the second half of the nineteenth century, having no churches of their own, the Armenian Apostolic Church advised them to be in touch with the Anglicans (Episcopalians), and to arrange to hold their services in Episcopal churches. But I digress. My ignorance of Armenians and Armenia was not fully corrected even at Yale, when I studied there in the 1960s. I overlapped in New Haven for two years with George W. Bush, but we ran in different circles and I never met him. By that time I had, however, met a few Armenians. Thinking back, I know I detected their strong sense of cultural heritage and national pride, but my curiosity had its limits, and I stayed well within them.

Given the total absence of Armenians from my world as I grew up in Tidewater Virginia, it was both instructive and surprising to learn that there had been an Armenian in precisely those parts in the seventeenth century. As the Senate Foreign Relations Committee considered my nomination to be the fifth U.S. Ambassador to the Republic of Armenia in 2004, I found myself telling Virginia Senator George Allen about "Martin ye Armenian," the first Armenian known to have come to the New World. Martin had been engaged by the Virginia Colony, a few miles upstream from my birthplace, in 1619, for the purpose of cultivating mulberry trees, on which silkworms feed. Another Armenian engaged in the same effort was known as George (his Armenian name was probably Gevork). As a boy I had climbed on the non-native mulberry trees – some of which still stand near the Colonial Capitol in Williamsburg – and was familiar with the Virginians' initial high hopes of producing silk, eventually dashed by the irresistible popularity and profitability of tobacco, but I had not known that an Armenian was the central figure of that effort. Our history is richer than we know. Certainly I had known next to nothing about the Armenians, but I was beginning my intellectual voyage: better late than never, given that I was headed to the Republic of Armenia in a matter of weeks.

So Who Are These Armenians?

The Armenians are one of the world's oldest peoples, identifiable as a distinct group as early as 500 B.C., according to mainstream historians, and even earlier according to some who claim that an Armenian "proto-nation" existed as early as the sixth millennium B.C. In confederation with the Urartians, the Armenians seem to have been present when the fortress of Erebuni was built in 782 B.C. on the outskirts of what is now Yerevan. Certainly the Armenians had emerged as a people by the time of the Behistun rock, erected by Darius I of Persia in about 520 B.C., which bears a reference to "Armenia."[*] There is certainly sufficient evidence to demonstrate that the Armenians were indigenous to the area geographers know as the "Armenian Highland" in eastern Anatolia, now part of the Republic of Turkey.

The classical historians Herodotus and Tacitus wrote about the Armenians and the ancient conquerors Xenophon and Alexander the Great actually encountered them. Armenians claim descent from Noah's son Japheth. According to Genesis, the Ark came to rest on Mt. Ararat, the mountain Armenians hold sacred.[†] In 301 A.D., the Armenians embraced Christianity as their state religion, the first nation to do so. Through the centuries, the Armenians' Christian

---

[*] Razmik Panossian, *The Armenians: From Kings and Priests to Merchants and Commissars*. New York, Columbia University Press: 2006, pp. 33-34.

[†] Mt. Ararat is visible from many parts of Yerevan, but is actually across the border, in Turkey.

Might one of the participants in the First Thanksgiving in 1619 at Berkeley Plantation on the banks of the James River have been Martin ye Armenian? (Painting by Sidney King used with permission of Berkeley Plantation).

faith has been at the center of their struggle to survive as a nation. In the early fifth century, the churchman and scholar Mesrop Mashtots invented the thirty-six-letter Armenian alphabet, which is still, with the later addition of two letters, used in Armenia today and is revered as a matter of national pride. In 451, at the battle of Avarayr, the Armenians were defeated by a superior Persian army intent on forcing them to submit and accept Zoroastrianism, the religion of their conquerors. The Armenian commander, Vartan Mamikonian, is a beloved national hero, and the battle is considered a victory because the Armenians, though subjugated, were allowed to retain their Christian faith.[*] Over the millennia, the Armenians' ancient Anatolian and Caucasian homeland suffered repeated invasions, by the Mongols, the Arabs, the Seljuks, the Persians and, most

* These events are the subject of a forthcoming film "East of Byzantium" by the director Roger Kupelian.

decisively, the Ottoman Turks. Bereft of a state of their own from 1375 until 1918, the Armenians found ways to survive as minorities in the Russian, Persian and Ottoman Empires and elsewhere. In the Ottoman Empire, and particularly in the capital city of Constantinople, the Armenians played an important and useful role as merchants, bankers, architects, officials and even diplomats, earning the epithet of the "loyal millet," (one of the semi-autonomous non-Muslim communities within the Ottoman realm). Reform efforts undertaken in the nineteenth century (the *Tanzimat*) first raised the hopes of Armenians for improved conditions of life. A relatively liberal constitution was adopted in 1876, but within a year the despotic and reactionary Sultan Abdul Hamid II prorogued the parliament, suspended the constitution and established autocratic rule. In the years 1894-96 the so-called Hamidian Massacres resulted in the deaths of as many as 300,000 Armenians. In the first years of the new century, both Turks and Armenians, the elite of whom had studied in Europe, sought greater freedoms and restoration of the 1876 Ottoman Constitution. When the Young Turks engineered a coup against the autocratic Sultan in 1908, Armenians and Turks together rejoiced at their success in moving the Empire forward to a constitutional order. This era of comity was to be short-lived, as a militantly nationalistic element of the Young Turks, organized as the Committee of Union and Progress (CUP), pursued policies that put them on a collision course with the Armenians. The European imperial powers, Britain, France and Russia, also manipulated the Armenian issue in the late 1800s and early 1900s, as they considered how they might profit from the impending collapse of the of the Ottoman Empire and maneuvered for advantage. The CUP took the Empire into World War I on the side of Imperial Germany. Beginning in 1915, the ruling Young Turks deported and murdered as many as one and one-half million Armenians in what virtually all historians and genocide scholars today agree was an act of genocide.

If you have an Armenian neighbor or colleague, the chances are good that he or she is a descendant of survivors of that tragedy. The

Genocide is the primary reason Armenians are here with us in North America in significant numbers. Nearly every Armenian family knows about the Genocide from its own experience and from stories told at home by an elder, perhaps a grand-parent or a great uncle. There is thus an enormous gap between the personal, direct knowledge the Armenians possess and the involuntary state of ignorance in which I, and so many other Americans, grew up.

It is not my purpose in this book to reexamine in detail the history of the Armenian nation or the Armenian Genocide, much less to present the results of new research. I am not a professional historian, just an amateur of sorts. The historical record has been amply documented by survivors, and by eye-witnesses, many of them American missionaries and diplomats, and examined elsewhere, by scholars far more knowledgeable than I, and the process continues apace. Several recent volumes by researchers with access to original documents in state archives have made the central facts of the matter quite clear, but have also unearthed new material that deserves further study. Readers who want to investigate the history of the 1915 Genocide for themselves may want to consult directly the books and articles discussed in Part II, many of which were instrumental in convincing me that I had a moral obligation to speak out on the issue. As for the question of whether the events should somehow officially be acknowledged as "genocide" by the United States, and what that would mean for all of us, I invite the reader to consider that question as I recount my own journey of discovery and crisis of conscience, and then to think through what can and should be done to deal with this issue. It is admittedly a terribly difficult one for all of us, Armenian-Americans, Turks and even for plain "unhyphenated" Americans, to the extent we know about it at all. And it is not simply going to "go away." The many young Armenian-Americans I have met at gatherings around this country, and the young generation of Armenians in the Republic of Armenia and in Europe and elsewhere will see to that. Increasingly, young Jewish-Americans are taking up the cause of their Armenian friends and insisting that Jewish community organizations drop their refusal – based on their understandable concern for Israel's defense relationship with Turkey – to acknowledge that the events of 1915 constituted a genocide that antedated and in some ways prefigured the Holocaust (in this connection, see the website Jewcy.com). It was, after all, a Polish Jewish lawyer, Raphael Lemkin, who, in 1944, coined the word "genocide," having in mind not only the Holocaust, in which so many of his own family perished, but the massacres of the Armenians a generation earlier. Most important, conscientious and brave Turkish scholars and researchers are now calling for a reexamination and reassessment of their own history. Resolving this matter will require the efforts of many different people, politicians, diplomats, public intellectuals, scholars and ordinary citizens and voters, including, one dares to hope, some readers of this book.

The question for all Americans, as for Turks and Armenians, ought to be how to deal with the issue in such a way that, like other horrific crimes of the past, it is properly recognized for what it was, so that some combination of contrition, justice and, eventually, reconciliation, can be achieved. The process has to start with knowledge. Because of my own ignorance of the history of the events of 1915-16, I had for years in a sense been a "denier" of the Armenian Genocide. However, as Henry Theriault has said, "a truly inadvertent denier will recognize the veracity of the genocide when confronted with the evidence."[*] It seems to me that all of us who have honestly been unaware of the historical facts surrounding the Armenian Genocide, including many Turks, can be excused for not knowing those facts. Likewise, not knowing the facts of what legally constitutes the crime of genocide as defined in the 1948 Convention is also an important factor for many of us who have inaccurate or incomplete information. But if we do know the historical and legal facts and

---

[*] Henry Theriault, "Denial and Free Speech: The Case of the Armenian Genocide," in *Looking Backward, Moving Forward: Confronting the Armenian Genocide*, Richard Hovannisian (ed.) Transaction Publishers: New Brunswick and London, 2003, p. 250.

persist in denying the truth, that is a different matter. Genocide scholars consider that denial is the last stage of genocide, the eighth stage, as Gregory Stanton has determined. If we deny the Armenian Genocide while possessing the historical and legal facts, we are in some sense, and to some degree, complicit.

The U.S. Foreign Service

At Yale, where I got interested in history, I decided I wanted to study more of it: nineteenth-century Russian History, to be precise. I had been especially fascinated by the period of the 1860s, when young students and romantic radicals in Russia dreamed of changing the Tsarist system. I was fortunate that Yale College in those years had a strong department of Russian Studies. The most popular lecturer on Soviet politics was Wolfgang Leonhard. Professor Leonhard had been a member of the East German elite and consequently knew the Moscow Communists, and their way of thinking, from direct experience. His lectures were literally standing-room-only. My favorite professor, though, was Firuz Kazemzadeh, whose father had been the Persian Ambassador in Moscow during the Stalin era, and whose mother was Russian. He had a wonderful, jovial, sly way of teaching history that inspired in me an interest in the Eastern influences on Russian culture and history. Under Kazemzadeh, I devoted my senior honors thesis to the student disturbances of 1861 in St. Petersburg. The student unrest in my own college years, 1968 in particular, piqued my interest in the student revolts of one hundred years earlier in Russia. I concluded on the basis of the Russian case that student revolution was ultimately doomed to failure: while students might have a momentary impact on public life, they tended to graduate, get married and start families, and quickly become a spent force. They have no staying power as a group. Student radicals sometimes do go on to make a difference, even if it turns out to be in banking or finance, but their impact tends to be gradual, cumulative and generational. I was not a student radical in college. In fact, I recall crossing picket lines of students (sociology majors for the most part) in order to reach my Russian language and literature classes. And yet, the atmosphere of the 1960s was impossible to ignore; we all wanted change, we wanted better government, we wanted honesty from our leaders.

Having traveled to the Soviet Union, Turkey (including Istanbul, 1966), and other parts of Europe, I thought I had a better sense of the world's realities than many of the student radicals of the 1960s. The Vietnam War was raging at the time. At one point, in 1968, I seriously considered applying for the Navy's Officer Candidate School in Newport, Rhode Island. I had drawn a low Selective Service lottery number, but a collapsed lung in my junior year rendered me decisively IV-F for purposes of the military draft. Although I opposed the Vietnam War, and signed more than one petition against it, I still wanted to serve my country in some active capacity. Through school friends I had heard about the U.S. Foreign Service. Most of my college classmates were headed for careers in the law or business. But we were, for the most part, a generation with a sense of public purpose. I remember vowing, with a handful of other classmates, that we would try to make a difference in the world, whatever we ultimately did for a living.

Imagining that Russian History was my calling, I applied to the PhD program at Columbia. After winning a Woodrow Wilson Fellowship, I enrolled in the History Faculty with the intention of becoming a scholar and teacher. Over the course of the first semester, though, I became disillusioned by the program. My professor, Leopold Haimson, was part of the problem. A grand bewhiskered presence who smoked cheroots like a true nineteenth-century Russian revolutionary – in fact, that was his background, his father having been a Social Revolutionary – Haimson was a great scholar. But the reality I faced was that that the PhD program did not even prepare one to be a teacher; rather, it was a research degree. My father had earned his doctorate, and I wrestled with the depressing prospect of not attaining an equivalent academic grade. In the end, with my father's good advice and support, I concluded that a life of academic

research was not really what I wanted, even if I could successfully obtain the needed credentials and land one of the few precious academic jobs then available in Russian Studies. Nor did I want to spend the next seven years breathing dust in Butler Library, as the PhD at Columbia typically required. So I arranged to see Prof. Haimson to discuss whether I ought to drop out of the graduate program. We met at a dingy café on Amsterdam Avenue. Almost the first thing Haimson asked was whether I had been to see "my analyst." My reaction was one of astonishment verging on horror; I had never consulted a psychiatrist and didn't think I needed one. Shortly thereafter I took the Foreign Service entrance examination in New York City. That year, there were some 18,000 applicants. I was one of the lucky three hundred or so who made it through the battery of written and oral examinations. Within a year, I was a newly-minted and very junior officer of the U.S. Foreign Service, grade FS-08, with an annual starting salary of slightly more than $9,000. I loved everything about this career, even the introductory training course, the famous "A-100" in which new officers were introduced to the mysteries and some of the traditions of American diplomacy. When it came time, toward the end of that obligatory A-100 course, to compete for foreign postings, I thought of what Professor Kazemzadeh had taught me, and put my name in for one position in Turkey (Izmir) and one in Iran (Tehran). Moscow was out of the question for new Foreign Service Officers in those Cold War days; it took me ten years to arrange to serve there. I was duly assigned to our Embassy in Tehran, given about four months of Farsi language training, and departed for Iran in early January 1972. It was there that my discovery of the Armenians, and ultimately, of their great tragedy, began.

Adventures – in Iran – with Turks and Armenians

My arrival in Tehran, aboard the old around-the-world Pan Am Flight 001, in the middle of the night, provided a surprise of a different sort from that which awaited me years later in Yerevan. As I

looked down on the approach to Mehrabad Airport, I thought Iran
must truly be a desert. There seemed to be so much sand below. We
landed, hard. The doors of the aircraft opened to a rush of frigid air.
What had looked like sand was in fact snow. Our winter landing had
been anticipated by a major blizzard. Ben Wickham, an affable
Foreign Service officer a few years my senior, met me at the airport in
his WWII-vintage Jeep and took me under his wing as I learned the
ropes of my job in the consular section, where he also worked. That
winter, living in temporary quarters at the U.S. Embassy compound,
I was nearly asphyxiated by a kerosene space-heater that
malfunctioned – as Iranian space-heaters are still doing – but
immediately I was up to my neck in work to protect American
Citizens' interests as a vice consul.

Iran under the Shah in 1972 was a far different place from what it is
today under the rule of the Ayatollahs and Presidents Ahmadinejad
and now Rouhani. For all his failings, Mohammed Reza Shah Pahlavi
was a strong and, in many ways, just ruler who did much to build his
country up. His father, Reza Shah, was cut from the same cloth as
Kemal Atatürk, the founder of modern Turkey. The Pahlavis were
respected by many, though feared by all. The Shah protected the non-
Muslim minorities, among them the Assyrians, the Armenians – the
most numerous Christian groups – and the Baha'is, a religious sect
with its origins in nineteenth-century Tabriz that is considered
heretical by Islam. Professor Kazemzadeh, my mentor at Yale, was a
senior member of the Baha'i faith, and I visited Baha'i meetings several
times in Tehran. The main minority groups in Iran, including most
notably the Armenians, by and large prospered under the Shah's rule.
They had their own schools, and lived normal, peaceful and generally
satisfactory lives. It is true, though, that the Shah's dreaded secret
police, the SAVAK, was hugely powerful in the pursuit of the His
Imperial Majesty's enemies. The number of his enemies grew over the
years. Although the definitive history of America's involvement in Iran
has yet to be written, it does seem clear with hindsight that we allowed
ourselves to be blindsided by our heavy commercial and strategic

interests to what was going on under the surface. I know, for example, that the Embassy's crack political officer, Stan Escudero, was twice warned by his superiors to desist from having tea with the bazaar merchants who were close to, and financed, the then-exiled Ayatollah Khomeini. Why? Because the Shah didn't want them talking to the Americans. We sold the Shah a tremendous amount of military equipment. As our political-military officer, Henry Precht, used to joke, "there's no business like Shah Business."

The American Embassy in Tehran employed many individuals from among these minority groups, so many Armenians, in fact, that some jokingly dubbed it "the Armenian Embassy." The Budget and Fiscal office of the Embassy was staffed almost entirely by Armenians. They were hard-working, honest, competent employees. The most famous Armenian in our employ was a short but very sturdy chauffeur, Haikaz Ter-Hovhanessian, the Ambassador's driver, mentioned above in connection with Haik, my driver in Armenia. I worked closely with him while serving as aide to the Ambassador. Haikaz had distinguished himself a few years earlier by cool-headedly maneuvering the Ambassador's limousine to safety during an assassination attempt carried out by two extremists armed with axes and an AK-47. Miraculously, after the 1979 Embassy take-over and the Islamic Revolution, he survived beatings and imprisonment inflicted simply because he had previously worked for the Americans. He eventually retired with a small pension. Years later, in the summer of 2006, I was amazed and delighted when Haikaz called the U.S. Embassy in Yerevan to tell me he was in Armenia. Now much older, but still sturdy and good-humored, he visited me at my office overlooking Mt. Ararat and we talked about old times and caught up on mutual friends. I gave him a ride back to his hotel in the Embassy's newly-arrived Cadillac. Still a professional driver at heart, Haikaz kicked the tires, looked under the hood and pronounced the limousine "a good one." Haikaz and I had come full circle after thirty years.

Consular work in the early 1970s in Iran was a fascinating introduction to diplomatic life, the Middle East and, especially, the realm of Shi'a Islam. As vice consul in charge of protecting Americans, I was sometimes called upon to identify the remains of fellow citizens who came to grief in one way or another in my consular district. My district included most of Iran (there were U.S. consulates also in Tabriz in the northwest and in Khorramshahr on the Persian Gulf coast, where Ryan Crocker, in recent times well known as the U.S. Ambassador in Iraq and Afghanistan, was also a vice consul). One of my first duties was to identify the badly-decomposed corpse of a young American woman who had ventured into the high mountains behind Tehran in the month of *Bahman*, which in Farsi means "avalanche" – and corresponds roughly with February. To this day I could not swear that the body I saw, which was disfigured beyond recognition except perhaps through dental records, was really that of the attractive young lady pictured in her U.S. passport. The circumstantial evidence was compelling, though, and I duly certified her death.

On another occasion, I traveled to the far eastern part of Iran, to the province of the holy Shi'a city of Mashad. We had learned in a crackly telephone call from local authorities that two young Americans had perished in a grisly collision with a oil tanker truck in the twilight hours when visibility on Iran's unlit rural highways was trickiest. The boy, nineteen, and his girlfriend, a year younger, had been riding a motorcycle from Kabul – and, as I later was to find out, probably using hashish. Their corpses were being held in a refrigerator in the office of the Public Prosecutor in Mashad. I had taken with me to Mashad a grizzled but wise old local employee of the consular section. He was my assistant and interpreter, an Azeri Turk by the name of Massoumzadeh. An awkward fellow with a limp but a twinkle in his eye, Massoumzadeh was the father of several daughters and one of the most sensible and worldly-wise of our employees. My job was to identify the bodies of my fellow countrymen, inventory their possessions, and tend to their local burial or shipment home for interment in the United States. Decisions needed to be made, and, as it turned out, both sets of parents were separated and living in various parts of the world, in Korea, Washington, D.C. and Latin America. This made communicating with them from remote Mashad difficult in those days of telegrams and telexes, long before the invention of e-mail. I had taken a certain amount of money with me, but, as it turned out, not enough to accomplish both a local burial and also an international shipment of remains. On account of the intermittent air connections to Tehran from Mashad, I had to give the parents a deadline by which they needed to decide whether they wanted to have the bodies shipped home – at their own expense, the U.S. Government not being a charitable organization – or interred locally. The estimated cost in those days of embalming and shipping two bodies from Iran to the United States was about $1300; local burial was cheaper. The deadline came and went. We had no instructions from the parents of the young victims. We continued waiting for two more days, but with new corpses showing up at the Public Prosecutor's Office, the local officials were understandably anxious about what we planned to do with the bodies. Even with clear instructions from the next-of-kin, we would need a bank transfer in order to send the young Americans' bodies home for burial. We reluctantly decided to move forward with local burial. It was at this point that the underlying religious realities came to the surface. Massoumzadeh did a remarkable job of finding a coffin-maker, grave-diggers and so on, but he pointed out one thing that was missing: this Muslim *Azeri* assistant told me we had to find an *Armenian* priest to administer last rites. We – or rather he – did find one, who agreed to come to the cemetery the next morning and officiate. It was a normal thing for my Shi'a Azeri assistant to know – and to insist – that we needed an Armenian priest in these circumstances. It was not an issue; this was the right thing to do, given that the young Americans were at least nominal Christians. The Armenian priest was the closest approximation we could find in that part of the world to a Protestant minister.

During the night prior to the planned burial, long after the decision deadline had passed, the parents of the deceased young

Americans finally reached us by telephone to say that they had decided they wanted the bodies of their loved ones sent back to the United States for burial. Unfortunately, no mention was made of cabling any funds for that purpose. The local burial was, alas, already set for six in the morning, shortly after dawn. Massoumzadeh and I raced into action. Although the Americans were officially, in fact and on paper, already buried, we could in good conscience do nothing other than to go hard into reverse. We sped to the cemetery to pay the grave-diggers and the Armenian priest. We persuaded highly dubious police officials to un-do the official paperwork, and, along the way, we stopped in to see the Public Prosecutor. He quickly took in the situation and lent us a huge sum of money (90,000 Iranian rials) to have new lead-lined coffins constructed to meet the higher international standards that had to be met for air shipment. Somehow, with the help of an ambulance equipped with a siren and flashing lights, we managed to get everything done before the last airplane left for Tehran at 0950 that morning. Massoumzadeh and I heaved huge sighs of relief as we saw the two regulation coffins loaded onto the plane just seconds before it took off, a delay of ten minutes having saved us from missing the flight. From Tehran's Mehrabad airport, in over 100-degree heat, I called the Embassy to report that we had arrived with two coffins and "needed a truck." My efforts in this case brought me to the attention of the Deputy Chief of Mission and I was soon asked to become aide to the new ambassador, Richard Helms, the former CIA Director, who had just been sent into productive diplomatic exile by President Nixon apparently for knowing too much about Watergate. Massoumzadeh got a pay increase. The Public Prosecutor had his loan repaid and his photograph taken with the Ambassador.

As a bachelor in Tehran on my first tour of duty, I had an enviable social life. Central to my popularity, I now realize with hindsight, must have been the institution of the American visa. Many evenings at the houses of well-to-do Iranians ended poorly, once it became clear to me that the unstated purpose of the dinner had been to probe

With my family at home.

for a visa issuance, usually a student visa. I also entertained frequently, in the ground-floor apartment, with rose garden and swimming pool, that I had rented in a building owned by an Armenian family, the Manuelians. They were punctilious, but fair and generous landlords. The only conflict I ever had with them was occasioned by one of their guests having parked in front of the garage, blocking my exit. Parking is always an issue, it seems, even though this was not Washington or New York, and it was not unheard of to have a camel come through our street. Years later I received a letter from the Manuelians' son, by then living in the United States, recalling that I had given him advice about applying to colleges in America. I recall drinking tea with the Manuelians on more than one occasion. I also knew many Assyrian Christians in those far-off Tehran days.

I was baffled by the Armenian language when I first heard it in Iran, although the Armenians I knew there spoke Persian, as I did. Eventually, when I began studying Eastern Armenian, an ancient Indo-European language, it was only with Persian (Farsi) that I found any similarities, loan words or cognates. On departing Tehran in 1974, I returned to the United States the long way around, through India, Thailand, Singapore, Hong Kong, the Philippines, Japan and Hawaii. As much as I loved Iran, I never went back, although I nearly managed to return and become a hostage in 1979. But that's another story, as, for present purposes, are my diplomatic assignments to Czechoslovakia, the Soviet Union, and NATO Headquarters in Brussels. It was in Brussels that I met Donna Chamberlain, a Canadian lady assigned to her country's delegation next door to the American Mission, and her daughter, Jennifer. They became my family and eventually American citizens when Donna and I got married. At the time, I was assigned to the Soviet Desk at the State Department in Washington, where my story resumes.

Earthquake!

In 1988 a tragedy put me again in contact with Armenians. In December of that year, Mikhail Gorbachev paid an official visit to the United States. Ronald Reagan was in his last days as President, and George H.W. Bush was due to be inaugurated the following month. General Secretary Gorbachev's visit to Washington had been a personal triumph for him and a high water mark for U.S.-Soviet relations. For those of us working on the Soviet Desk at the State Department, Gorbachev's departure for New York was a cause for celebration – but then, on December 7, a tragedy occurred in Soviet Armenia: a huge earthquake.

The Director of the Soviet Desk, Mark Parris, had been deeply involved in the just-concluded Gorbachev visit to Washington and still had to transcribe his notes of the meetings, so it fell to me as his deputy to take charge of the issue of what to do about the earthquake in the Soviet Union. First reports were sketchy, but as more information arrived, the extent of the terrible damage and human casualties became clear. It was an awful disaster. But the earthquake also presented a timely and unusual diplomatic opening. In the friendly aftermath of General Secretary Gorbachev's visit, President Reagan offered U.S. assistance to the U.S.S.R. and Gorbachev accepted. This was unheard of during the Cold War and marked a milestone. The Chargé d'Affaires of the Soviet Embassy in Washington, Evgeniy Kutovoy, followed up diplomatically by officially requesting help, but by then the wheels were in fact already turning. The late Julia Taft, then the energetic head of the Office of Foreign Disaster Assistance, had already sprung into action, and was busy organizing rescue teams, complete with sniffer-dogs, from Fairfax County, Virginia, to fly to the stricken Soviet Republic of Armenia. So urgent was the task at hand that we sent the first aircraft toward the U.S.S.R. without obtaining final flight clearances, and our personnel aboard that flight – the first of about thirty-five – lacked Soviet visas. I called one young officer on the staff of the Soviet Desk, Aubrey Carlson, at home that evening at about seven o'clock. I instructed him to be at Dulles Airport at ten with warm clothes and a small bag: he was going to Armenia to help with the earthquake relief. To his credit, Aubrey never questioned the need abruptly to leave the comparative comfort of Northern Virginia at the Christmas season to do what had to be done. For the next two weeks, we communicated by the only means available in that pre-cellular time: by means of a field satellite dish set up in the earthquake zone near Leninakan (now Gyumri). Aubrey later received a well-deserved award from the Armenian government for his service there.

My involvement with the earthquake required me to work with Armenian-Americans in the United States as they pulled together as never before to aid their fellow Armenians in Leninakan and Spitak. I recall addressing a fund-raising event in New York at which all the bishops and archbishops of the Armenian churches were present, their differences momentarily forgotten. My job was to advise the Armenian-American community on what the Federal Government

North and South Caucasus.

was doing, what our people on the ground –Aubrey Carlson and Ross Wilson (later U.S. Ambassador to Baku and Ankara) – were reporting, and to suggest useful things that private Armenian-American groups could do to help. I also was later given an award – a bronze medal – by the authorities in Soviet Armenia, although my role had been far less significant than either Aubrey's or Ross's.

The terrible earthquake was an important moment in many respects. As each day brought new headlines in the Washington *Post*, we saw a progression: at first the quake was "Soviet; then it was placed in "Soviet Armenia;" finally, it was pin-pointed in "Armenia." I believe that through this tragedy, many Americans of my generation first learned where Armenia was, just as many television viewers first learned from the tsunami on Boxing Day, 2004, where Indonesia and the Maldives were. Certainly the 1988 earthquake brought the Armenian-American community together in a new way, and with new urgency. Many young members of that community first visited Armenia in connection with earthquake relief efforts and had their first real exposure to the country at that time.

It was also an historic turning point in the Cold War: the first time humanitarian assistance had been offered by the United States to the Soviet Union, and accepted by the latter. In addition, it marked the beginning of the United States' deep involvement in Armenia in our own times. That early humanitarian effort eventually grew into the heavy involvement in economic development that we see today. For the Armenian-American community also, it was a moment of self-awareness and mobilization, as recorded in such accounts as Carolann Najarian's *A Call from Home.*[*] And finally, the earthquake was a critical turning point within the U.S.S.R. General Secretary Gorbachev, when he left New York to fly first to Moscow and then to the stricken area, was met by a disenchanted public, distressed not only about the inefficiency and insufficiency of Moscow's assistance efforts, but also about its ethnic policies in the region. Earlier in the year, the Soviet (legislative assembly) of Nagorno-Karabakh, a predominantly Armenian enclave in neighboring Azerbaijan, had voted to transfer its allegiance from the Azerbaijani S.S.R. to the Armenian S.S.R. This move had set off deadly riots in the Azerbaijani port city of Sumgait in which three dozen or so Armenians perished. While these ethnic clashes (and others that took place in Baku in 1990) cannot accurately be characterized as "genocide," they were an early signal of further trouble. As we now can see with hindsight, the nationality problems that were poorly addressed in the Russian Empire and not adequately dealt with in the Soviet Union (initially by Josef Stalin, the Bolsheviks' Commissar of Nationalities) would worsen in the *perestroika* era and continue to plague regional stability long after the "Evil Empire" had disappeared.

* Carolann Najarian, S. *A Call From Home: Armenia and Karabakh: My Journal* (Cambridge, MA: Arpen Press, 1999).

Opening to the Ottomans

In the wake of my work on the Soviet Desk, I was selected by a State Department Awards Committee to receive a Una Chapman Cox Fellowship for the academic year 1989-90. Una Chapman Cox was a lady of means from Texas. Impressed by the dedication of an American diplomat while traveling overseas, she donated a considerable portion of her fortune to establish the Una Chapman Cox Foundation. The Foundation supports the U.S. Foreign Service in various ways, including by awarding one or two Cox Fellowships each year to allow individual Foreign Service Officers to pursue special projects or a course of study. I applied for a Cox Fellowship to investigate an idea first advanced by Timothy Garton Ash, namely, that the Soviet Union might disintegrate in a manner not unlike the decline of the Ottoman Empire. He called his hypothesis the "Ottomanization" of the U.S.S.R.[*] but did not develop it much further. I set out to explore the metaphor, delving into Ottoman history in search of possible common elements that might enlighten our understanding of the forthcoming Soviet collapse. At the Kennan Institute, which generously provided me with an office, I concentrated on the nineteenth-century Ottoman reforms, collectively known as the *Tanzimat.* There I first grappled with the "Armenian Question."

The fall of 1989 was not the best time to be pursuing academic study. That was the autumn in which the Berlin Wall came down and the Soviet hammerlock on Eastern Europe began to weaken. The quick succession of events that led to the dissolution of the Soviet Empire undermined Garton Ash's Ottomanization thesis, with its assumption that the process might be messy but gradual. Things happened so quickly that, half-way through the year, the State Department asked me to return to work to coordinate a number of conferences being planned by the Conference on Security and

---

[*] Timothy Garton Ash, "The Empire in Decay"; The *New York Review of Books*, Sept. 29, 1988. Others had predicted the decline and fall of the Soviet Union, but without using such an evocative metaphor.

Cooperation in Europe. I did what I could to complete my research, hastily presenting it to a Wilson Center audience as "Ottomanization in Fast Forward" at a noon discussion in the Castle of the Smithsonian, but then I moved back to the State Department. My article, overtaken, and its hypothesis disproven, by events hugely dissimilar from those that marked the long and stately, but ultimately violent, Ottoman decline, was never published.

What I gained from my semester's study of Ottoman history was a general familiarity with the issues, especially of the last century of Ottoman rule, and a sense of their richness and complexity. I remember reading that the Armenians of Anatolia were viewed with distrust as early as 1825 by their Turkish overlords, for their affinity with Orthodox Christian Russia. One of the standard texts I read, Lord Kinross's *The Ottoman Centuries: The Rise and Fall of the Turkish Empire,*[*] dealt rather fully and straight-forwardly with the 1895-96 massacres of Armenians under Sultan Abdul Hamid II,[†] but devoted only two sentences to the more notorious events that the world knows as the Armenian Genocide of 1915, the narrative dissipating into a hurried review of the end of World War I and the fall of the House of Osman. Yet even these two sentences by Lord Kinross, who was in general highly sympathetic to the Turks, were telling: he noted that the British defeat at Gallipoli left the Young Turks free to pursue their "premeditated internal policy for the final elimination of the Armenian race" and that the Armenians' "proximity to the Russians on the Caucasus front furnished a convenient pretext for their persecution, on a scale far exceeding the atrocities of Adbul Hamid, through the deportation and massacre of one million Armenians, more than half of whom perished."[‡]

---

[*] Lord Kinross, *The Ottoman Centuries: The Rise and Fall of the Turkish Empire.* New York: Quill, 1977.

[†] On the Hamidian massacres, see Arman J. Kirakossian, *The Armenian Massacres, 1894-1896: U.S. Media Testimony,* Detroit: Wayne State University Press, 2004, with Forward by former Senator Bob Dole.

[‡] Kinross, p. 607.

Another history of the period that I read at that time, *The Rise of Modern Turkey,*[*] strikes me today as inadequate in its treatment of the Armenian Question. Its conclusion is that the "…Armenians also feel that the deaths resulted from a planned policy of genocide by the Ottoman government. This accusation was repeated by several European commissions during and after the war. The Ottoman cabinet records, however, do not confirm this…" The authors of this work, Stanford J. and Ezel Kural Shaw, do not give sufficient attention to the role of the extra-governmental *Teşkilat-i-Mahsusa* (Special Organization), which we now know was responsible for much of the violence perpetrated against the Armenians, and their work does not reflect what we now know about how genocide happens. To their credit, the Shaws did leave a place-holder for future historians, noting that "considerable further study is needed to determine the exact degree of blame and responsibility that can be assigned to each of the parties involved."[†]

Much of the important research on the Armenian Genocide has been done only in the last twenty-five years, and in 1989, there was much less available to the general reader. Ottoman history, with its fantastic richness and variety, is unfortunately not taught in any but a tiny few of our schools. It is partly for this reason that ignorance and even denial of the Armenian Genocide have been possible in the United States. Today, with the important historical and interpretive works that are already on library shelves and with more important scholarly volumes, by Armenian, Turkish and other scholars, in the offing, the previously prevailing public ignorance is becoming less widespread and the excuses for not knowing about an important historical event are becoming steadily less tenable.

The scholarly assessment of the events of 1915 has become so much clearer that in 2008, Yale historian Jay Winter could write of

---

[*] Stanford J. Shaw and Ezel Kural Shaw, *History of the Ottoman Empire and Modern Turkey, Volume. II: Reform, Revolution and Republic: the Rise of Modern Turkey, 1808-1975.* Cambridge University Press, 1977.

[†] Ibid., p. 316

Turkey's "refusal even to countenance the word 'genocide' to describe the extermination of approximately 1 million Armenians." Winter went on to say that "in a way, the Turks are still fighting World War I and trying to defend the honor of the Kemalist revolution that gave birth to modern Turkey by denying a crime that everybody with eyes to see accepts as historical truth."[*] All this was not so clearly evident, at least to me, when I first dipped into Ottoman history in 1989. I was still mired in at least relative ignorance of the historical record, woefully uninformed about the genocides of the twentieth century and only dimly aware of the 1948 Convention on the Prevention and Punishment of the Crime of Genocide that had been ratified by the U.S. Senate in 1988.

An Ambassador Prepares

When I next returned to the subject of Ottoman history and the Armenian Genocide, it was under wholly different circumstances. After diplomatic postings in Czechoslovakia – which became the Czech Republic and Slovakia as a result of their "velvet" divorce – in the early 1990s, and to St. Petersburg, Russia, in the second half of the decade, Donna and I had returned to Washington. But then I accepted an assignment to head the Mission to Moldova of the Organization on Security and Cooperation in Europe, which was attempting to mediate between the recognized government in Chisinau and the separatist regime in Tiraspol, across the Dniester River. It was challenging work with an international civilian and military staff, and I returned home with even more fluent Russian, having had to conduct all business, including daily staff meetings and press conferences, in that language. While I was in Moldova, Donna had had to fend for herself in Washington. She did well, becoming in time President of the World Affairs Council there, and running a remarkable array of programs for the organization's members and a

---

[*] In a review of *Where Have All the Soldiers Gone?* by James Sheehan, in The *American Prospect*, April 17, 2008.

special outreach to the District of Columbia schools. I came back
from Moldova to head an office of the State Department's Bureau of
Intelligence and Research, and, after 9/11, was asked to take on the
Directorship of the Office of Russian Affairs. But by the summer of
2003, Donna and I we were ready to head out again on a foreign
assignment. About that time, we were excited to learn that I would be
nominated as America's next ambassador to Armenia, with a likely
departure in the summer of 2004. Although I had started my Foreign
Service career in Iran, and had visited Tabriz, just across what was
then the Soviet border, my wife and I had never been to Armenia. We
had come close: in April, 1996, President Clinton, after a highly
successful visit to St. Petersburg while I was Consul General, had
asked the State Department to find me an ambassadorship. State
proposed me for Baku, the capital of the Republic of Azerbaijan. In
the end, this did not work out, and the post instead went to my old
friend Stan Escudero, who had served in Iran under the Shah. At the
time, we had been excited about Baku, and read all the literature we
could find about Azerbaijan. Now we were just as excited about
Yerevan.

There is nothing in the career of a Foreign Service Officer and in
the life of his or her family that compares to the thrill of knowing that
one is headed for the highest level of honor and responsibility an
American diplomat can aspire to: to represent his country as an
ambassador. The process of preparing for an ambassadorial
assignment is arduous, involving a lengthy background investigation
and security clearance, a full financial disclosure and other hurdles
that must be cleared, including some sixty pages of forms to be filled
out. Much of this preparation has to be accomplished during the pre-
confirmation period, even before the nomination is made public by
the White House, and every effort must be made to avoid the
appearance of assuming that the Senate Foreign Relations
Committee, and ultimately the full Senate, will accede to the
President's choice, although in the case of career officers they rarely

fail to do so. I eventually cleared all the hurdles and the White House announced my nomination on May 4, 2004.

A shortcoming in the preparation of ambassadors arises from the need to avoid assuming one will be confirmed by the Senate: official, government-provided training – in the language, the history and culture of the future host country – is normally not offered until *after* the confirmation process is complete, at which point time is very short. Other Foreign Service officers assigned to embassies, for example, political and economic section chiefs, even deputy chiefs of mission, typically receive a year of training in the language and area studies, yet it is the ambassador who will be facing the press and other audiences every day and could profit from such training most of all. It can be argued, of course, that the ambassador has a professional staff to advise him on such matters. That is indeed true, but in practice insufficient, as an ambassador will many times be out on his own and unable to consult his staff. When I asked for some training in Eastern Armenian – the language spoken in today's Republic of Armenia – I was told, "don't bother; you'll never learn it; just go out there and use your Russian."

One of the best sources of advice for new ambassadors is other ambassadors, who have "been there" themselves and know what the job really entails. It was thus a great satisfaction for me to connect with former Ambassador to Syria and Israel Ed Djerejian, for whom I had once worked in the Moscow Embassy, and who, as Director of the Baker Institute at Rice, contributed heavily to the work of the Iraq Study Group. As a young Foreign Service Officer of Armenian background, Ed had once been trotted out to meet the lone Armenian Soviet Politburo member, Anastas Mikoyan, when he visited the State Department. Ed told the story in a hilarious, self-deprecating way. But now he gave me good advice about Armenia. He had kept up to date and had solid instincts about the leadership. I talked at some length also to my immediate predecessor in Yerevan, John Ordway, and to his predecessor (another old friend), Michael Lemmon.

My confirmation hearing before the Senate Foreign Relations

Committee was set for June 16. As was traditional, I sought meetings with key Senators, notably Senator Sarbanes of Maryland, who was influential on Armenian issues, prior to my hearing. I was to be reviewed by the Committee along with Charlie Ries, scheduled to serve as our ambassador to Greece, and Tom Korologos, set to become ambassador to Belgium. Senator George Allen of Virginia chaired the session, which was notable for the appearances of Senators McCain, Byrd, and Hatch in support of the nomination of Tom Korologos, a legendary Republican lobbyist, known affectionately as "the 101st Senator." Tom and his wife Ann were favorites of Donna's and mine, and gave us lots of good advice about the confirmation process, in which Tom was expert. In the event, the introductions and amusing stories about Tom Korologos took up nearly all of the one hour allotted to the hearing. The room was packed with Tom's relatives and friends, because, as Tom laughingly put it, "Korologoi travel in packs." Charlie Ries and I later joked about our "big fat Greek hearing."

As it turned out, the Senators had no questions for Tom Korologos or Charlie Ries, but I got a couple of questions in the last five minutes of the one-hour session that I easily answered. I knew enough at that time to say something about the issue of the Genocide, without, however, breaching the taboo on the "G" word. Here's what I said: "Long before the present-day Republic of Armenia arose from the ruins of the Soviet Union, the people of the United States sympathized with the plight of Armenians who suffered and perished in the declining years of the Ottoman Empire." It was not much, but I hoped that my words at least conveyed to my listeners a recognition that something awful had happened in those years, and that we knew it. Helpfully, Senator Sarbanes "instructed" me to learn Armenian. Armed with the Senator's words, I went back to the State Department and asked to have as much training in Armenian as the calendar would allow before my departure. State relented and issued orders enabling me to have eight half-days of instruction in Eastern Armenian. While this hardly produced fluency, it did enable me to learn the alphabet and to pronounce a few phrases and short sentences. The full Senate voted to confirm my nomination on June 25, and we scheduled our departure for late August of 2004.

Although I had cleared the bureaucratic obstacles, I was still woefully deficient in my knowledge of Armenian history and culture. I decided, now that I was officially confirmed and could afford a short breather, to retreat to our daughter's house in Sag Harbor, on Long Island, and read Armenian history intensively for the first half of July, in lieu of a crash course on the subject. I borrowed or bought all the books I could locate, and read compulsively, aided by a stretch of rainy Long Island weather. Michael Lemmon, my predecessor-once-removed as ambassador in Yerevan, loaned me his copy of *Ambassador Morgenthau's Story*,[*] as well as Richard Hovannisian's two-volume *The Armenian People from Ancient to Modern Times*.[†] I purchased Peter Balakian's prize-winning *The Burning Tigris: The Armenian Genocide and America's Response*[‡] at Borders. Annie Totah had given me a copy of the large-format paperback volume that replicates the reports that appeared in the New York *Times* during the war years.[**] I also had with me Gerard Libaridian's *Modern Armenia: People, Nation, State*,[††] and Thomas de Waal's excellent volume on the Nagorno-Karabakh conflict, *Black Garden: Armenia and Azerbaijan Through Peace and War*,[‡‡] as well as a number of other

---

[*] Henry Morgenthau, *Ambassador Morgenthau's Story*. New York: Doubleday, Page and Co., 1918, Reprinted 2016 London: Gomidas Institute.

[†] Richard Hovannisian (ed)., *The Armenian People from Ancient to Modern Times*, Two Volumes. New York: St. Martin's Press, 1997.

[‡] Peter Balakian, *The Burning Tigris: The Armenian Genocide and America's Response*. New York: Harper Collins, 2003.

[**] *The Armenian Genocide and America's Outcry: A Compilation of U.S. Documents, 1890-1923*, n.p.: Armenian Assembly of America, 1985.

[††] Gerard Libaridian, *Modern Armenia: People, Nation, State*. New Brunswick, NJ: Transaction, 2004.

[‡‡] De Waal, Thomas, *Black Garden: Armenia and Azerbaijan Through Peace and War*. New York: New York University, 2003.

materials provided by the State Department, including transcripts of earlier Congressional hearings about the so-called "Events of 1915."

It was *Ambassador Morgenthau's Story*, primarily, that first convinced me something was terribly wrong about the way we were treating the issue of the Armenian Genocide. The fact that Morgenthau, himself a Jew, and the U.S. Ambassador to Constantinople at the time the events occurred, had dubbed the massacres and deportations an "attempt at race murder" was arresting. That his consuls, Leslie Davis and his contemporaries, had also seen with their own eyes things that seemed since to have been forgotten, was also compelling. I felt a distant kinship with my diplomatic forebears, a solidarity with them over the decades, and a gnawing sense that the United States had somehow betrayed their legacy. But I certainly did not know what could or should be done in the present day, or how to go about it. I realized only that the issue was taboo in the State Department, *utterly taboo*. I was perplexed and troubled, but also, at this point, terribly rushed; time before our departure for Armenia was now short. On our return to Washington in mid-July, I turned to preparing systematically for my assignment, and began extensive consultations with virtually everyone in Washington who had anything to do with the Republic of Armenia, and with the Armenian-American organizations that represented the Armenian-American community; "Team Armenia," I called them. On July 29 the Bureau of Intelligence and Research, where I had worked on post-Soviet issues, organized a full day's seminar intended to educate me on current issues, inviting such scholars as Gerard Libaridian and Fred Starr to make presentations. I also managed (thanks to Senator Sarbanes) to spend eight half-days studying Eastern Armenian with Karine and Diana Saponjian at the National Foreign Affairs Training Center at Arlington Hall (which former Secretary of State Shultz, to his lasting credit, had secured for training our diplomats). There was virtually no time to look deeply into the issue of the events of 1915, although a long and serious lunchtime conversation with Robert Krikorian, of the State Department's Office of the Historian, introduced me to the work of Raphael Lemkin, the Polish Jew who first coined the word "genocide" in 1944 and led the effort to enact the 1948 Convention on the Prevention and Punishment of the Crime of Genocide. Lemkin lost some forty-nine members of his family in the Holocaust, but the original impetus to define the crime to which he gave the name "genocide" was in fact the earlier episode in which the Armenians of Anatolia were nearly annihilated during World War I.[*] A lawyer in the Office of the State Department's Legal Adviser also helped me to understand the background and current status of the issue. All my conversations on this topic were somewhat furtive because it was understood that it was not something one was meant to discuss.[†]

Although the troubling question of the Armenian Genocide was simmering in the back of my mind, it did not prevent my wife and me from preparing for our assignment to Yerevan. One of the most challenging and enjoyable parts of being assigned abroad as ambassador is that the State Department's Art-in-Embassies Program is available to help select a collection of American art works to be displayed in the official residence. Donna and I loved folk art, and had already begun collecting naïve representations of Adam and Eve in Prague and St. Petersburg. What we found intriguing about the works of art depicting humanity's first couple was the way naïf artists in different cultures handled a universal theme. One Polish "Adam" in our collection sported a Lech Walesa mustache, for example. A Czech "Adam" bore a curious resemblance to Vaclav Klaus, Prime Minister during our time in Prague. But there was another, more serious reason to choose American folk art, with an emphasis on Old Testament themes, for our official residence in Yerevan. We wanted to demonstrate our country's affinity for the deep religious roots that

---

[*] On Lemkin, see especially Samantha Power's account in *"A Problem from Hell": America and the Age of Genocide*, chapters two and three.

[†] In testimony June 18, 2008 to the House Foreign Affairs Committee, Assistant Secretary of State for European Affairs Dan Fried claimed that the topic was no longer off limits in the European Bureau.

From my swearing-in ceremony, 11 August 2004.

the United States shared with Armenia. And, in the aftermath of the scandal at the Abu Ghraib prison in Iraq, we wanted to project a distinctly conservative cultural image. The curator of Art-in-Embassies, Virginia Shore, clearly more drawn to "insider art" of the kind one typically finds in public buildings in New York and Los Angeles, gamely cooperated with us in identifying some works she probably considered "retro" or at least "outsider" art. Virginia introduced us, through a catalogue entitled "An American Eden", to the world of Earl Cunningham, a "vernacular" artist whose works were nearly all in the collection of the Mennello family of Florida. Eventually, the Mennellos generously lent us five Cunninghams to display in our official residence in Yerevan. These paintings on masonite, simple scenes of coastal life as the artist remembered it from Maine to Florida, became the backbone of our small collection. The culturally conservative art exhibit was enriched by an 1830s embroidered sampler of Adam and Eve, a watercolor entitled "Jacob's Dream" by Malcah Zeldis, and a whimsical wooden model of Noah's Ark by the Hispanic folk artist Luis Tapia lent by the American Folk Art Museum in New York.

Deputy Secretary of State Richard Armitage swore me in as the fifth U.S. Ambassador to the Republic of Armenia on August 11, 2004. By happy coincidence it was Donna's and my wedding anniversary. Donna held my late mother's Bible as Mr. Armitage administered the oath of office.[*] I recall his remarks well, because, most graciously, he thought to praise my wife, who was once again giving up her job, this time as President of the World Affairs Council of Washington, in order to accompany me abroad. The Deputy Secretary dubbed us "Team Evans." Both Armitage and his good friend and immediate boss, Colin Powell, were hugely supportive of U.S. diplomats and their families, and were enormously popular with the Foreign Service. Some weeks earlier, we had had our photo

---

[*] I had confided to my mother, just before she died in February 2004, that I was to be named Ambassador to Armenia. She may not have understood exactly where Armenia was, but she gave her blessing.

snapped with Secretary Powell. Donna and Powell quickly hit it off, and the photograph shows him and her broadly smiling. I looked strangely grim. Probably I am the only person in history who has failed to beam for the camera while being photographed with Colin Powell. For me, it was a deeply serious moment.

The crowd of guests in the Treaty Room on the Seventh Floor of the State Department included a number of Armenian-Americans we had met, or who were known to the Armenia Desk. In my remarks, I asked the guests to "picture if you will a state, smaller than many but larger than some, surrounded by four other states, with one of which, to the northeast, there is a history of border disputes. Picture further, if you will, a landscape of mountain lakes, of beautifully situated churches that bear witness to an ancient faith and reveal a genius for architecture. And consider that this state used to extend, in the West, all the way to the sea, before war and the encroachments of other states reduced it to its easternmost component, as it exists today... I refer, of course, to my home state of *Virginia*..." The Treaty Room resounded with startled laughter as I continued, "...where, as early as 1619, was living a certain Martin ye Armenian." I proceeded to tell the story of Armenian involvement in Virginia's ill-fated attempt to cultivate silkworms in the seventeenth century. This was my way of saluting both my home state and the country of our impending assignment, but also of emphasizing two serious points: that Armenians and Americans have interacted over many centuries, and that the glories of the past often, in both the Old World and the New, give way to the scaled-down realities of the present.

The Background Notes

My last meeting before departing Washington for Yerevan was with Ambassador Elizabeth "Beth" Jones, the Assistant Secretary of State for European and Eurasian Affairs. A Swarthmore graduate, Beth had served in the Foreign Service slightly longer than I. She was and is one of America's most distinguished diplomats, who did an excellent job in her time leading the European Bureau. During the first part of

With Secretary of State Colin Powell.

her tenure, it fell to me to brief her daily on events in the former Soviet Union, while I was in charge of analysis for that part of the world in the State Department's Bureau of Intelligence and Research. Later I worked for Beth as Director of the Office of Russian Affairs. It was to her, primarily, that I owed my appointment as ambassador to Yerevan. In our meeting, slightly truncated by an urgent telephone call she had to take, Beth agreed with me that the State Department "Background Notes" on the Republic of Armenia ought to make some mention, albeit using already approved and cleared language, of the 1915 massacres of Armenians in the Ottoman Empire. I had noticed that the publicly available Background Notes on Armenia, which students and general readers were in the habit of consulting in great numbers, were entirely silent on the subject. They left the reader with the misleading impression that nothing at all untoward had happened in that year, or in any year, for that matter. It had also come to my attention that this omission was being routinely justified by the State Department, in letters to outraged Armenian-Americans, on grounds that "there is not enough space on the website to deal with every issue." There were things we *could* say, drawing on the President's April 24 Proclamation on Armenian Remembrance Day. Not to say *anything* was, I thought, devious and especially offensive to Armenian-Americans who counted themselves among the descendants of Genocide survivors. Beth had just agreed with me that the Notes* ought to address all major issues of interest to our "customers." Then her telephone rang. I left Beth's office believing I had her approval to work to amend the Notes as we had discussed. The Armenia desk officer, Eugenia Sidereas, a talented and energetic young Foreign Service Officer, participated in the conversation and witnessed Beth's agreement with my point. But this project took a back seat while I proceeded to take up my new assignment.

Presenting Credentials

One of the ancient traditions of diplomacy is the presentation of credentials, or "letters of credence," to the Head of State of the receiving country. This is a way of ensuring that the arriving ambassador is in fact who he claims to be: the genuine representative of the sending state. In a modernized version of this procedure, I presented xeroxed copies of my credentials to Foreign Minister Vartan Oskanian on Monday, August 23, the first working day after my arrival; this allowed me to meet the Foreign Minister, who is typically the ambassador's most important and frequent interlocutor. Vartan greeted me warmly and immediately suggested that we be on a first-name basis. An Aleppo-born Armenian, the descendant of Genocide survivors, Vartan had studied at the Fletcher School of Law and Diplomacy at Tufts and had given up his U.S. citizenship in order to serve the new Republic of Armenia after its independence. He had already proven his worth as Armenia's chief representative, developing an enviable reputation with other foreign ministers around the world. Vartan's fluency in English, as well as French and

---

* Background Notes can be viewed at *www.state.com*, but are no longer being produced or updated.

Arabic, gave him access and credibility that some of his colleagues in other post-Soviet states clearly lacked. After our first meeting, Vartan enthusiastically participated in the ceremony of swearing in our Peace Corps volunteers that afternoon. Word quickly came that I was to present the originals of my papers to President Kocharian on September 4, the Saturday before Labor Day. The Chief of Protocol reviewed with me and the DCM[*] the details of how that formal ceremony would proceed. It involved my going, at the appointed hour, to the Presidential Residence on Baghramian Avenue, a few buildings up the street from what was then the American Embassy, accompanied by the key members of my staff, the same group that had met me at the airport a few days earlier. It would be televised, and, from that moment forth, I would officially be recognized in Armenia as the U.S. Ambassador.

For my presentation of credentials, I learned to say a few short sentences in Armenian. At the same time, I began meeting all sections of my Mission staff. My first "Town Hall" meeting with the entire staff – we had about 320 Armenian employees and 70 Americans – took place in the auditorium of our old chancery, a former Komsomol (Communist Youth Union) building, on August 27. Aided by our shy, but tireless, interpreter, Tigranuhi Baghdasarian, I outlined my vision for the Mission as a whole and asked for everyone's assistance in carrying out my own duties as Ambassador. I recalled that, when I had been awaited as U.S. Consul General in St. Petersburg, the question asked by apparently anxious Russian employees was "does the new Consul General drink?" By contrast, the question the local Armenian employees had been asking was "does the new Ambassador have a sense of humor?" I think the question spoke well of the Armenians at the Embassy and I hope it answered itself. One question – from an American employee – at first struck me as some sort of a provocation: "if you were on the far side of Lake Sevan and needed to get to the other side, how would you proceed?" I pondered this briefly, and answered roughly as follows:

* Deputy Chief of Mission Anthony Godfrey.

"if you rearrange the letters of my last name, you will see that they spell 'SEVAN'." That seemed to answer the question; at least it would work well on a map. I had the feeling that this group was going to be fun to work with, as well as a challenge, in a good sense.

On the appointed day, I met with President Kocharian and presented my credentials in accordance with the protocol requirements, even pronouncing a few short Armenian sentences fairly well before stumbling toward the end. There followed a formal conversation over Armenian coffee about current events and my views of U.S.-Armenian relations. I outlined our policy in the South Caucasus as being based on three pillars: supporting the stability and security of the young states, building their economies, and strengthening their democratic institutions. For his part, President Kocharian bore down on the issue of the closed border with Turkey.[*] He wanted my thoughts on what the economic burden, or cost to the Armenian economy, was, and what the effect might be of reopening it. I had read a number of estimates of the cost, from an early one which put it at nearly 50% to other, more recent, estimates that saw the cost as having declined because free markets had found ways to get around the closure. Kocharian noted that in the early years of the Republic of Armenia, it may actually have been helpful to Armenia for the border to be closed to Turkish competition, as it provided *de facto* protection to fledgling Armenian producers on the domestic market. But Kocharian thought that the time was coming when Armenia would need to look beyond its own markets to the wider world.[†]

---

[*] Turkey closed its border with Armenia in 1993 in solidarity with Azerbaijan during the Karabakh war.

[†] It is inaccurate to term the closure a "blockade," although the intent is similar. Goods and people move in both directions through Georgia or Iran, or by air. The effects of opening the border were exhaustively examined in a special issue of the *Armenian Journal of Public Policy*, ISSN 1829-0027 (Feb. 2007).

I invited my senior colleagues back to our residence for champagne right after the ceremony of presentation of credentials, and we celebrated the start of our work together. It was Labor Day weekend for us Americans, so I didn't detain my colleagues long. All of them had family or other obligations. So far, things had gone extremely well, but Donna and I needed a break from the intense Yerevan heat. We headed to alpine Lake Sevan for the long weekend, booking a room at the Tufenkian Hotel at Tsapatagh on its northern shore. This turned out to be one of our favorite haunts. Though not directly on the beach, the hotel, and especially its stand-alone restaurant, commands a wonderful view of Lake Sevan and its ever-changing weather. As it happened, that weekend the hot, arid weather that had been gripping Yerevan since our arrival began to break. A tremendous thunderstorm crossed the lake in full view, followed by remarkable effects of the sun and even a double rainbow. Donna and I marveled at the stormy weather and light effects on Sevan for what must have been several hours. When the storm had passed, the summer weather was finished for that year.

We also had a sobering experience at Tsapatagh. We had asked our driver to find the local church. He reported back somewhat shame-facedly that the village had originally been Muslim: there was therefore no church. On a later visit to Tsapatagh with friends, we discovered a cemetery in which Muslim gravestones had been knocked down. Populations had been transferred, at times by violent means, in this part of the world. We did not have the whole story and could not testify as to what exactly had happened here. But it seemed clear that everyone was in some way a victim of a terrible shared history.[*]

---

[*] Unfortunately, the desecration of cemeteries has not ended. In late 2005 there were credible reports, including a videotape, of the destruction of the Armenian cemetery at Old Jugha in the Nakhichevan exclave of Azerbaijan, apparently by men in Azerbaijani army uniforms. See the report of the multi-national Caucasus Reporting Service of the Institute for War and Peace Reporting at www.iwpr.net.

Exploring Armenia

In succeeding days and weeks, I called on all the leading officials of the Republic of Armenia, from the Prime Minister (the late Andranik Margarian) to the then-Speaker of the National Assembly, Artur Baghdasarian, to the Chief Justice and cabinet ministers. Each of these conversations was useful for general background, but also to press the U.S. agenda. My strategy was to move outward in concentric circles, from the center of power – the President – through the ministers and eventually toward the more far-flung provinces (*marzes*) and governors (*marzpets*). I also called on His Holiness Karekin II, the Catholicos of all Armenians, at his official seat at Etchmiadzin. I found Karekin to be a most engaging and down-to-earth churchman of intelligent and remarkably modern outlook. He was assisted by a young, married Armenian-American priest, Father Ktrij Devejian, from Fresno, who proved to be an important link to the Catholicos as well as a valued friend and interpreter to all who would listen of Armenian Christian theology and traditions.

It is a diplomatic tradition for newly-arrived ambassadors to call on their already-established colleagues in the diplomatic corps, the other ambassadors. Although this custom is frequently observed in the breach nowadays, I have always felt it made good sense and helped to establish comity and better understanding among diplomats. I made a point, therefore, of calling on all of my ambassadorial colleagues, except for the Iranian (with whose government we did not have relations), starting with the Russian, Anatoliy Dryukov, who, as the longest-serving member of the Corps, was its *doyen* or "dean." I officially called on him September 9th, but two days earlier I had signed the condolence book at the Russian Embassy for the tragedy at the school in Beslan, in North Ossetia, only a few days before, and had thus met him briefly. Ambassador Dryukov was one of the most effective and likeable of Russia's diplomats. At that time, he had been in Armenia for nearly five years. We quickly developed a rapport, and, in the course of our initial conversation, established our mutual adherence to a principle our predecessors had also agreed upon: that Russian and American interests were not in fundamental conflict in Armenia. We both wanted to see a prosperous, democratic and secure Armenia, at peace with its neighbors. If there were any major differences, they had more to do with how to deal with Iran than with support for the Republic of Armenia.

There was one more thing the Russian Ambassador and I could fully agree upon, and that was our governments' determined opposition to terrorism. In the wake of the tragedy at the school in Beslan, I invited my Russian colleague to join the American community and well-wishers in our own tribute, on September 11, 2004, to the victims of the attack on the World Trade Center three years earlier. Ambassador Dryukov agreed then and there, and did not let me down. He came to our event, a short theatrical performance by deaf and mute actors at the Theater of the Young Viewer, and spoke movingly of our tragedy and his. A few risk-averse members of my staff did not approve of my having invited the Russian Ambassador to join "our" commemoration without having first obtained Washington's approval, but I proceeded in the firm belief that terrorism is an evil no matter who its victims, and that combating it – and honoring its victims, of whatever nationality – transcended national lines. Dryukov spoke so movingly at the event that my impromptu invitation to him was vindicated in the eyes of my skeptical staff.

In this same initial period, I was invited to breakfast with the American Chamber of Commerce, an association of business-people with citizenship or business ties to the United States. My wife had been involved in setting up the American Chamber in Prague when we were there, and we put great value on getting to know these influential and well-informed entrepreneurs. That morning I met the Chairperson of the Chamber, Edith Khachaturian, a young lawyer from San Francisco of Armenian background, born in Iran. We hit it off immediately and chatted and joked in her fluent – and my rusty –

Farsi. Other members of the Board of the American Chamber included another Armenian-American "re-pat," the lawyer Tom Samuelian, who later became dean of the law faculty at the American University in Armenia. Yet another was a Briton, Jonathan Stark, who represented an important Armenian-American investor and philanthropist, Gerry Cafesjian, and had married a charming Armenian lady. The Chamber became for me a valued sounding board, and we routinely arranged for visitors from Washington to meet with its members, especially prior to the semi-annual sessions of the U.S.-Armenia Economic Task Force. The Task Force was an inter-governmental commission that had been established to keep track of official U.S. economic assistance programs and Armenia's progress toward meeting economic and democracy goals. By the time I served in Armenia, cumulative American assistance to that country had reached $1.6 billion, not an enormous amount, but enough to put Armenia's *per capita* receipts among those of the top three or four countries in the world, Israel and Egypt being first and second. After the short Russian-Georgian conflict in August, 2008, the Republic of Georgia ranked among the top recipients as well.

Early in my tenure, I asked to be briefed in depth on the various programs of assistance that the U.S. Government was carrying out in the areas of business development, energy, water use, public health, and democracy building. I asked Robin Phillips, the wise and experienced director of the USAID Mission – a part of the overall U.S. Mission, but proudly distinct from the Embassy as such – to set up back-to-back briefings on all aspects of our programs. Robin had been born in Egypt and raised in Taiwan. He had studied economics at Stanford, Harvard and the London School of Economics. Perhaps this, and long service in USAID, gave Robin the confidence to let his Armenian local staff conduct the briefings with minimum interference from him or his American deputies. I was greatly impressed by the depth and breadth of knowledge the USAID staff possessed. I had been told prior to arriving that the Armenian employees of our Embassy in Yerevan might well be the best-educated such group in the world. Surely I had no reason to doubt it after hearing this battery of presentations, delivered in excellent English, with minimal preparation and maximum effect. This was a hugely competent and effective group of professionals, ably led and highly motivated.

Those Background Notes!

Now that I was establishing myself in Yerevan, I reverted to an issue that had figured in my last conversation in Washington with Assistant Secretary of State Beth Jones. During the fall of 2004, I several times asked the Armenia Desk about amending the Background Notes* to reflect at least some minimal awareness on the part of the State Department that a tragedy – we did not necessarily have to call it "genocide," – had befallen the Armenian people in 1915. The answer, from the Deputy Assistant Secretary level, repeatedly came back roughly as follows: the European Union is considering whether to set a firm date for starting negotiations with Turkey about the latter's accession to the EU; now is not the time to amend the Background Notes on Armenia. I was told to wait until after the European Summit on December 17.

In the meantime, a high-level group of Armenian-American visitors sponsored by the Armenian Assembly of America visited Yerevan. I briefed them at the Marriott Hotel Armenia, and answered one question about the Armenian Genocide. I did so in the standard way, starting off by noting that "no American official has ever denied the facts of what happened in 1915," then quoting verbatim from President Bush's most recent April 24 statement which regretted the "annihilation of as many as 1.5 million Armenians through forced

---

* The State Department Background Notes are brief descriptions of the countries with which the United States maintains diplomatic relations. They contain short histories of the countries, descriptions of their political systems, and information of interest to students and travelers.

exile and murder at the end of the Ottoman Empire"* and avoided
uttering the "G" word. The gentleman who had asked the question
was not in the least satisfied. He was emotional. In a plaintive tone,
he asked, "why is it that I had no grand-parents and no aunts or
uncles?" I had no good response to that question. The audience had
good manners and did not attack me personally. They understood I
was sticking to the official version of events, and to the official
characterization of them as "mass killings," "forced deportations" and
even "murder," while avoiding the forbidden term "genocide." I had
before me an audience of Armenian-Americans who knew their
history, many from the direct testimony of their relatives, others from
intensive study. The issue, and the tension it provoked, was palpable,
but my own private reaction was to promise myself that I would look
into the matter more thoroughly.

This was, by the way, virtually the only time the question of
American policy toward the Genocide was raised with me publicly in
Yerevan, where standards of journalism are different from our own.
No local Armenian journalist ever asked me directly about the
Genocide, although an Armenian-American journalist from Los
Angeles did so at my first press conference (I ducked her question).
Polls have consistently shown that Armenians living in the Republic
of Armenia have numerous concerns that take precedence over
Genocide recognition by the international community, although
such recognition is definitely something they would like to see. The
issue *is* on the foreign policy agenda of the Republic of Armenia, but
is *not*, as is sometimes erroneously claimed, a *precondition* to
establishing normal diplomatic relations with Turkey. Turkey's
position has, unrealistically, included a demand that Armenia stop
seeking international recognition of the Genocide.

December 17, 2004 came and went: the European Union decided
to move ahead with talks with Turkey about its accession to the EU.
Biding my time, some weeks later I inquired again about amending

---

* President Bush's Proclamation on Armenian Remembrance Day, April
24, 2004.

the Background Notes, and was told that it was now "too soon after" the European Union decision to consider amending the Notes. It dawned on me that, in the view of my superiors at the State Department, *there was no good time even to make the minor, fully-cleared addition to the Background Notes – based on the President's own language – that needed to be made!* I had collided with a permanent taboo, which rested on a perpetual – and likely unalterable – calculus in favor of Turkey's official position and against the legitimate claims of history and of the Armenians. The balance of interests in favor of Turkey at the State Department was subtly reinforced in 2004-05 by the fact that Beth Jones's deputy, Deputy Assistant Secretary Laura Kennedy, whose area of responsibility included not only Turkey, Greece and Cyprus, but the Caucasus and Central Asia, had served in Turkey and Turkmenistan. Her successor, Matthew Bryza, had a Turkish partner.[*] There was no way to fight City Hall, even when they were my old friends. But, personalities aside, given the permanent balance of U.S. interests in favor of Turkey, a nation of some 72 million, with which the U.S. has important defense and economic relationships, it seemed to me there was no way that the question of the Armenian Genocide would ever adequately be dealt with. We certainly could, and should, have done a better job of addressing the concerns of our Armenian-American fellow citizens by at least taking a version of the existing language, sanctified by having already been issued as a Presidential Proclamation, and deploying it effectively in the Background Notes. The situation appeared to me to be hopeless and destined to remain so endlessly. I was frustrated. But the issue was not just going to go away. I felt strongly that someone had to do something, and when I looked up and down the chain of command, that "someone" probably had to be me. No one else cared about the issue or was in a position to do anything about it. At that point, even I myself was not ready to address the question head-on. It took further reading and soul-searching for me to reach the point of

* Zeyno Baran, whose work as an analyst in Washington is well known. They married in August 2007.

breaking publicly with the official policy of my government. After more than thirty years in the Foreign Service, I could not take such a decision in haste or without considering the potential consequences for United States interests and for myself and my family.

It was not simply the fact that my superiors at the State Department were deaf to my pleadings that the Background Notes needed revision that put me on a collision course with U.S. policy; the Notes are important because they are consulted by school children and students, but they are hardly a major vehicle for policy articulation. It was the underlying issue that put me on the horns of my terrible dilemma: essentially, the U.S. policy of tacitly denying that a "genocide" had occurred in 1915 placed me in the position of having to misrepresent, when the question came up – as it certainly would during my upcoming speaking tour of Armenian-American centers in the United States – the historical and legal facts as I now had come to know them from my own intensive program of study. The policy was forcing me to prevaricate, or at the very least to engage in convoluted and unconvincing reasoning. It was the tension between what I now knew and the official policy that was forcing me to choose. The fact that even the lowly Background Notes were considered immutable simply multiplied my frustration.

Other U.S. diplomats, faced with this issue, have come out in a different place. Ambassador Mort Abramowitz, while serving as envoy to Turkey in the early 1990s, once lobbied some sixty Senators not to support a resolution then pending in the Senate that would have recognized the Armenian Genocide as such. Years later, though, he recalled that "[it] was, I confess, a bad moral dilemma for me because of the massive killings of Armenians at that time."[*] Abramowitz, one of our most distinguished diplomats, did what was expected of him, and I do not condemn him, or any of my other colleagues who have done likewise. To his credit, Ambassador Abramowitz demonstrated, in the interview cited, a keen sense of the ethical dilemma he faced.

---

[*] Interview by Alan Honley in the *Foreign Service Journal*, July-August, 2006.

My critics have asked why I did not, at this point, resort to the Dissent Channel. The Dissent Channel was, and remains, a kind of policy safety valve. It was originally established during the Vietnam War era to enable dissenters within Foreign Service ranks to raise policy issues outside the normal chain of command. I should probably have aired my concerns about the non-recognition by the United States of the historical and legal facts of the Armenian Genocide in that special channel. But I had the impression that the authors of Dissent Channel cables received, at best, and in the fullness of time, polite brush-offs, written by members of the Secretary's Policy Planning Staff, that were cleared with the relevant policy bureaus, that is, the same people who would not even consider amending the Background Notes for Armenia to acknowledge that "something unusual" happened in 1915. The bureaucratic equivalent of a Maginot Line stood resolutely in unthinking defense of the current policy.* It frankly did not even occur to me to use the Dissent Channel: the outcome was too obviously predictable. In any case, I would have to face the issue one way or the other during my speaking tour of Armenian communities in the United States, which was coming up very soon.

There was another consideration. The issue of the Armenian Genocide was not a typical foreign policy question to be politely debated in a morning staff meeting; nor was it open to some artful give-and-take, perhaps to be tasked to an interagency group, treated in a memo or two, with the result that all could be worked out and the policy "tweaked." No, the Armenian Genocide was a moral issue, a big moral issue, maybe not for everyone, but certainly for me as the U.S. Ambassador to Armenia. The case for recognizing the Armenian Genocide as such could probably not then, or perhaps ever, have been made on traditional *Realpolitik* foreign policy grounds alone. Turkey was too powerful and too important; it presumably always would be. The Republic of Armenia, land-locked and poor, lacking in energy or

---

* As noted, this situation may now have changed somewhat for the better: Assistant Secretary Fried told a Congressional committee June 19, 2008 that the question could now be discussed in the European Bureau.

other natural resources, would never loom very large in Washington's foreign policy calculus, although it had in Woodrow Wilson's time, on account of the Genocide, in fact. No, the argument had to be made in terms that transcended the normal arithmetic of national interests available to us as Foreign Service professionals. It had to be made on moral and ethical grounds. And to be heard, it had to be made public. But something else also affected my thinking at this time.

A "Track Two" Breakthrough

"Track Two Diplomacy" is what we call efforts by private groups or individuals to explore possibilities and options in situations where official diplomacy either has failed or for some other reason cannot produce the desired outcome. Pioneered by John McDonald, Joe Montville, and others in the 1970s in the Middle East, "Track Two" efforts have had a mixed record of success. During my first six months in Yerevan I became aware, from a talented member of the Embassy staff, an Armenian-American native of Pasadena, Aaron Sherinian, of the work that had been carried out in 2001-2004, with funding from the Department of State, by the Turkish-Armenian Reconciliation Commission (TARC), under the leadership of David L. Phillips.[*]

The TARC had commissioned a legal analysis through the International Center for Transitional Justice (ICTJ) in New York, which contracted with a private legal authority, as of this writing still unidentified.[†] The main findings of the ICTJ were two, which can be summarized as follows: First, the study concluded that the 1948

---

[*] David Phillips has recorded the story of TARC in his *Unsilencing the Past: Track Two Diplomacy and Turkish-Armenian Reconciliation*, New York: Berghahn Books, 2005.

[†] Mr. Paul van Zyl of the ICTJ explained to me on April 30, 2007 that the author(s) of the report were not identified so as to avoid personal attacks on them by either side. He also assured me that the analysis was truly driven by the legal material itself and not fashioned to conform to a preordained political agenda.

Genocide Convention could not be applied retroactively to the events of 1915 and that "…no legal, financial or territorial claim arising out of the Events could successfully be made against any individual or state under the Convention." However, the study also concluded that, despite many disagreements about what had happened in 1915, all of the four elements of the Convention's definition of the crime of genocide had been met: "(1) one or more persons were killed; (2) such persons belonged to a particular national, ethnical, racial or religious group; and (3) the conduct took place in the context of a manifest pattern of similar conduct directed against that group." Concerning the fourth element, that of intent, the ICTJ analysis found that "at least some of the perpetrators of the Events knew that the consequence of their actions would be the destruction, in whole or in part, of the Armenians of eastern Anatolia, as such, or acted purposively towards this goal, and, therefore, possessed the requisite genocidal intent." It concluded by saying that "*the Events, viewed collectively, can thus be said to include all of the elements of the crime of genocide as defined in the Convention, and legal scholars as well as historians, politicians, journalists and other people would be justified in continuing to so describe them.*"[*]

TARC was – and remains – controversial, especially among Armenian-Americans. Some distrusted the State Department's motives in organizing it. The mere fact that it was initiated by Under Secretary of State Marc Grossman, a former U.S. Ambassador to Turkey, made it suspect from their point of view. Others resented the manner of its announcement, with little or no advance consultation with Armenian-American groups, notably the Armenian National Committee, which was kept at arm's length from the TARC's proceedings. Although the product of this group's efforts had been criticized both by Armenians and by Turks, I believed it represented

---

[*] *Legal Analysis of the Applicability of the United Nations Convention on the Prevention and Punishment of the Crime of Genocide to Events which Occurred During the Early Twentieth Century*, Turkish Armenian Reconciliation Commission, Trilingual Edition, Rockville, MD: September 2004.

solid analysis and pointed the most reasonable way forward toward eventual reconciliation between the two communities and the two states. What it conspicuously lacked was a robust "truth" component along the lines of Archbishop Desmond Tutu's "Truth and Reconciliation" commissions in post-apartheid South Africa, in which the basic bargain was "truth for amnesty." President Bush's April 2005 proclamation praised the TARC study, while noting that it "does not represent the last word" on the matter.[*]

My discovery of the TARC's legal analysis was a crucial milestone on my journey toward recognizing the 1915 "Events" as an act of genocide and deciding to do something about it. That the TARC study was referred to in the President's 2004 Proclamation gave me further reason to believe it constituted a major breakthrough. I am not the only one to have reached this conclusion: in an open letter to the governments of Turkey and Armenia dated April 9, 2007, fifty-three Nobel Laureates endorsed the basic finding of the legal analysis: that the "Events of 1915" included all elements of the crime of genocide, but that, at the same time, the 1948 Genocide Convention could not be used to press territorial or other claims against the modern-day Republic of Turkey.[†]

I was not yet aware that there was a different school of thought on the matter of responsibility and applicability of the 1948 Convention, most effectively articulated by Alfred de Zayas, a Harvard-trained lawyer and former Secretary of the U.N. Human Rights Commission now in Geneva. Mr. de Zayas had argued that the Genocide Convention did not create a new crime under international law, but was "declaratory of pre-existing international law." De Zayas went on to argue that there was no time limitation on its prosecution. He anticipated a counter-argument, that the Republic of Turkey was not a

---

* I do not presume to supply the "last word" on this vexed issue either, but readers may want to give TARC's *results* a second look. Sometimes a bad marriage can still produce worthy offspring.

† The full text of the Nobel Laureates' letter is available at *www.eliewieselfoundation.org*.

party to the Convention on the Non-Applicability of Statutory Limitations to War Crimes and Crimes Against Humanity, by asserting that international law was clear: "there is no prescription on the prosecution of the crime of genocide."[*]

De Zayas makes a strong case, and his argument is elegant, particularly when he sidesteps the question of the 1948 Genocide Convention entirely and argues that "the Armenian claims derive from the doctrine of State responsibility for crimes against humanity... which predated the entry into force of the Genocide Convention;"[†] however, one can easily imagine international lawyers quarreling endlessly, and fruitlessly, about whether the 1948 Genocide Convention is, or is not, applicable retroactively and how other elements of "pre-existing law" would be applied so long after the events of 1915.[‡] My own opinion is that both the ICTJ finding and Alfred de Zayas's approach are valuable to have on the table. Indeed, de Zayas's arguments have a definite moral weight and cannot be simply dismissed; my problem is not with him or with them. Yet I think the overall question of the Armenian Genocide is likely to find its ultimate resolution not in any single court proceeding or legal action (such as a parliamentary resolution), but in a much broader context that depends on the internal politics of Turkey, diplomatic steps undertaken by Turkey, Armenia and Azerbaijan, as well as the European Union and the United States, civil society and public opinion in each of the countries involved and world public opinion. The position of the State of Israel is also especially significant, given both its political weight and its unique historical connection with the Holocaust.

---

[*] This means there is no limitation on its prosecution.

[†] De Zayas, Alfred. *The Genocide Against the Armenians, 1915-1923 and the Relevance of the 1948 Genocide Convention.* Beirut: Haigazian University Press, 2010, p. 44.

[‡] Mr. Paul van Zyl of ICTJ stressed to me that the ICTJ analysis addressed the applicability of the 1948 Convention *only*, a point that is made clearly in the text of the memorandum as well.

Speaking Frankly

In preparation for the speaking tour of university campuses and Armenian-American communities that had been scheduled for February of 2005, I did further intensive reading in Armenian and Ottoman history. By coincidence, our daughter's marriage was breaking up in New York, and my wife, Donna, had departed Yerevan to be with her, leaving me with unfilled evenings and weekends that I devoted to reading more about the Genocide issue. I studied Samantha Power's *A Problem from Hell: America and the Age of Genocide,*[*] which begins – powerfully – with the Armenian case. I also read the volume edited by Jay Winter, *America and the Armenian Genocide of 1915.*[†] And I studied Harut Sassounian's straightforward and handy *The Armenian Genocide: Documents & Declarations, 1915-1995,*[‡] from which I first learned, to my surprise, that President Ronald Reagan had used the term "genocide" in a statement he issued in April 1981.[**] Although there was no place in my Embassy briefing book for the question of the Genocide, I was nonetheless fully read up on it, thanks to these authors and my own intensive program of study. These authors and their writings were persuasive. My decision was ripening in the quiet of my sunlit upstairs library in Yerevan. It was not a pleasant feeling, more of a foreboding that I was destined to violate a taboo respected by my Foreign Service colleagues. I knew by this time what I believed, but frankly did not know yet what I would ultimately do with the knowledge I now so unhappily possessed. As impious or impertinent as it might seem, I privately sympathized and identified

---

[*] Samantha Power, *"A Problem from Hell": America and the Age of Genocide.* New York: Perennial Books (reprinted by arrangement with Basic Books), 2003.

[†] Jay Winter, ed., *America and the Armenian Genocide of 1915.* Cambridge: Cambridge: University Press,: 2003.

[‡] Harut Sassounian, *The Armenian Genocide: Documents and Declarations, 1915-1995.* 80th Anniversary of the Armenian Genocide Commemorative Committee. Los Angeles: 1995. This volume was updated and revised as *The Armenian Genocide: The World Speaks Out* in 2005.

[**] Ibid., p. 20.

with Adam in the Garden of Eden, having tasted of the fruit of the Tree of Knowledge; thanks to our collection of folk art, Adam and Eve stared out at me from our walls as a reminder of that sad and prophetic tale.

People have asked me at what exact point I decided to employ the word "genocide" in speaking to Armenian-American and university audiences during that February 2005 trip. I did not use the word in my appearances in New York (at the Archdiocese of the Armenian Apostolic Church), or in New Jersey, where I visited the Hovnanian School, a private Armenian school that emphasizes achievement in the humanities and the arts. It was directly after visiting the Armenian Museum and Library at my next stop, in Watertown, Massachusetts, which boasts a small, but superb, permanent exhibit on Armenian history and culture, including the Genocide, that I first uttered the word publicly.

I had, by that time, thought long and hard about the historical facts as well as the political effects of the U.S. Government's position of apparent neutrality – but of *de facto* support for Turkey – on the matter. It seemed to me clear that, with the issue permanently "off the agenda" of the State Department (not to mention the Department of Defense, with its enormous stakes in the military relationship with Turkey) there was no way to move forward. No one above me in the hierarchy would risk questioning policy, nor could anyone below me. I concluded that, as the U.S. Ambassador to Armenia, I was the only one who could realistically do anything to move the issue off dead center. Someone had to step "outside the box" in order to shake things up and cause them to move. If I did not act, years could pass and no progress would be made.

There were other things that weighed on my decision process. About this time, the *Wall Street Journal* published an Op-Ed[*] about the pressure that was being brought to bear on my fellow U.S.

---

[*] "The Sick Man of Europe – Again" by Robert L. Pollock, *WSJ* of February 16, 2005. Mr. Pollock is a senior editorial page writer at the *Wall Street Journal.*

ambassador in Ankara, Eric Edelman, on account of his religion, among other things. Eric is of Jewish background, although he is married to a Christian lady and does not wear his religion on his sleeve. Like Henry Morgenthau before him, Eric knew he was representing the United States, and not only American Jews, in Turkey. Eric's Turkish detractors, though, had seized upon Eric's Jewish background and were, at least according to the *Wall Street Journal* Op-Ed, deriding him and making his life miserable. On March 17, doubtless for a mixture of reasons, he resigned his position as U.S. Ambassador and announced his retirement from the Foreign Service. While this news was not directly related to the Armenian Genocide, it filled me with indignation at the biased – not to say anti-Semitic – media treatment Eric had been subjected to.

A further consideration was that Secretary Powell had – correctly, in my view – officially labeled the continuing massacres in Darfur a case of "genocide" in testimony before the Senate Foreign Relations Committee on September 9, 2004. If the Secretary could use the word for an ongoing, continuing, contemporary horror – to which the 1948 Genocide Convention certainly did apply – why could not the State Department find it in its heart *just to use already-cleared language – the President's own words* – in the Background Notes on Armenia? After all, those events had taken place some ninety years ago, but were definitely still an issue that cried out to be addressed, even if the dreaded word "genocide" was not employed. It just did not make any sense to me.

In the end, I decided to breach the taboo, gingerly at first, always making it clear to my American audiences that I was expressing my *personal* view, and that the *official* position of the U.S. Government *had not changed*. On each occasion, in Watertown, at UCLA, at Fresno, and at Berkeley, I attempted to explain the reasons for U.S. policy, rooted as they were both in solidarity with a long-time NATO ally, Turkey, and in Washington's high hopes for what secular Turkey might do over the long run in the Greater Middle East. I recalled for my listeners my experience at a conference of intelligence analysts I had participated in, at Wye Plantation on Maryland's Eastern Shore, at which Turkey's critical location and potential as a bridge to the troubled Middle East had kept coming up as a pivotal factor for the future of U.S. policy in that region. I also explained to Armenian-American audiences that, in the view of most experts, the Genocide Convention was not retroactive, and that the insistence of some of their number on pressing extreme territorial and other claims against Ankara tended to excite Turkish nationalists and make the linked issues of Genocide recognition and Armenian-Turkish reconciliation even more intractable.

Long after my trip, Harut Sassounian located a videotape of my remarks to an Armenian-American audience February 18, 2005 at the Holy Trinity Armenian Apostolic Church in Fresno. It was made by an elderly gentleman, and I was not even aware that I was being taped. Harut transcribed from that videotape one of my responses:

> I accept your challenge. Let me first of all say that no American official has ever denied the events of 1915. In fact, the State Department archives are filled with Ambassador Morgenthau's reports, and the reports of his consuls, some of which had to be sent to him in code, because the Turks at that time were interfering with diplomatic communications. I have done a lot of reading. I have done some study of Ottoman history a few years back. When I learned that I was being assigned to Yerevan, I went and read Ambassador Morgenthau's book. I read also Prof. Richard Hovannisian's two-volume history. I read several other accounts of what I will say tonight was clearly an act of genocide.
>
> Now let me briefly be very clear about what I have just said. I have called "the thing" by its name. It's a very painful experience, I know, for everybody, and I think almost all Armenian families, who didn't have the good fortune to fetch up on these shores before 1915, have been in some way affected by it.
>
> I used "the word" tonight because that's what it was. If you look at the criteria of the 1948 Convention on

Genocide, it fits. Before I went to Yerevan, I went and talked to the Legal Department of the State Department. There is one lawyer there who has the unhappy job of dealing with the issue of genocide, past and, unfortunately, present. I asked him, "isn't it the case that, had the Convention been in force in 1915, it would have fit these criteria?" He said, "yes." Now, the one element, if you look at the criteria in the Genocide Convention, the one element which has been elusive is the element of "intent," which has to be there.

I know that many of you may have heard of the flawed TARC process – the Turkish Armenian Reconciliation Commission. It was funded by the State Department. I am ready to admit that this process was undoubtedly flawed. I talked to David Phillips, who has just written a book about it. But what they did achieve in that process was a legal opinion that, indeed, those events should be called a genocide. At the same time, the lawyers who looked at this pointed out that the Convention was not in force at the time and cannot be applied retroactively. So, while we may call it that, there are some provisions in the Convention which cannot be applied. The general rule of international law is that conventions are arrived at by the states which sign them and they bind those states for the future. They do not have retroactive effect. I also know that there are some international lawyers who disagree with that. But the bulk of the international legal opinion is that a convention of that sort cannot be applied retroactively.

I would be remiss if anybody left this room tonight believing that the United States Government has changed its policy with regard to the application of the Genocide Convention. It has not. But I am committed to dealing with this issue as honestly forthrightly and sensitively as we can. I believe we owe it to each other, as fellow Americans, to discuss without playing games, without playing "gotcha."

Now someone can go out of this room tonight and distort what I have said, and I could lose my job. I know that I am taking a risk because I am ahead of some other elements of the U.S. Government in my treatment of this. But I am deeply convinced that I am doing the right thing in leveling with you about this issue.

I think ninety years is too long for us not to discuss the issue and call things by their own names.[*]

Armenian-American audiences to whom I spoke that February night applauded my remarks, but were apparently caught psychologically off guard. Although they were gratified to hear me use the forbidden word, and realized that something highly unusual was being said, most of my listeners understood that I was not reflecting the official position of the U.S. Government on the issue. Indeed, I had clearly stressed that I was expressing my personal view, but of course I was effectively challenging the official position. By using the term "genocide" in the first six months of my ambassadorship, rather than as a cheap "parting shot" on my way out, I was forcing the issue onto the public agenda. I knew full well that this could cost me my assignment and maybe even my career. But voices within me, dating back, no doubt, as far as my mother's simple instruction always to "tell the truth," and later training in "situational ethics"[†] at St. Andrew's, counseled that someone – either I or eventually someone else – had to step forward and tell the truth. The French diplomat, François de Callières, in his *On the Manner of Negotiating with Princes*, had written, "Honesty is here and everywhere the best policy,[‡] and I had always

---

[*] Transcript courtesy of Harut Sassounian, who printed it verbatim in his column of Feb. 22, 2007.

[†] Situational ethics, as I was taught it, interpreted moral principles in their context. In a famous example, traceable to Samuel Johnson and Cardinal Newman, if a murderer asks which way his intended victim went, lying may be an appropriate response. Sissela Bok's *Lying: Moral Choice in Public and Private Life* (New York: Vintage Books, 1979) is a comprehensive view of the question of the ethics of deception, and makes the important point that deception on the part of public officials undermines public trust, which ought to be considered a "social good to be protected just as much as the air we breathe." (p. 28)

[‡] As quoted by Charles W. Thayer, in *Diplomat* (New York: Harper & Brothers Publishers, 1959), p. 47.

believed that for a diplomat knowingly to voice an untruth was a professional, as well as an ethical, error of the first order. My action was, to some extent, an act of self-sacrifice. My own fate was not the important thing. The State Department could disavow my words, clarify them, or even recall or dismiss me. Still, a message would have been sent, to whomever was listening, that there was a serious problem here, and that not all American diplomats were uninformed or inclined to mislead. Although ninety years had passed since the events themselves, someone had to engage in "up-standing," as Samantha Power defines the act of refusing to be simply a passive "bystander." My words were definitely not a slip of the tongue. Rightly or wrongly, I had now gone public with my views on the Armenian Genocide, and would have to pay a price. How high a price would be demanded, I did not yet know.

Confession

I returned to Washington from my speaking tour and promptly reported to Deputy Assistant Secretary of State Laura Kennedy that I had breached the taboo on what is still, somewhat coyly, called "the G word." I reported my transgression to Laura before she read about it as reported in the Armenian-American press by Roxanne Makasdjian of the Armenian National Committee in San Francisco. Although I explained that I had used the word in an historical, not a legal, sense, and had taken care to specify that I was expressing my own view, which differed from the official one, this news was not well received. I was soundly rebuked, but Laura nonetheless invited me to take part in bilateral consultations that same day with a visiting Turkish official, Ambassador Halil Akinçi, Director General of the Turkish Foreign Ministry for Bilateral Political Affairs. The U.S. side was instructed not to raise the issue of the Armenian Genocide. But Amb. Akinçi himself raised it – and in the same breath denied that it had happened – stating, I thought quite outrageously, that "we all create the history that we need," and "there was no genocide; many of the Armenians escaped; if we [Turks] had really wanted to do away with them, we would have used machine guns and bullets." The Americans all sat there, speechless, during this unexpected outburst. I think it made everyone on our side of the table, and not only me, uncomfortable. No one took even the smallest issue with Akinçi's assertions. Before the session broke up, I privately told him that the foreign ambassadors in Yerevan would like nothing more than to have a Turkish colleague. This was a sincere statement, but my real message to him was that Turkey and Armenia ought to establish diplomatic relations. As indeed they should.

This Turkish official's attitude to the matter only confirmed my sense that the established American policy of tolerating the Turkish position was harmful not only to the truth, but to the prospects of encouraging the Turks to reconsider their own past. Without significant pressure from the outside, those courageous voices inside Turkey that were struggling to make it a more democratic and self-critical society would be at the mercy of Turkish ultra-nationalists.

I had faced calculations of this sort before, from another angle. In Communist Czechoslovakia in the mid-1970s, it had been my job to cover domestic politics and the dissident movement. The outstanding event of my tour in Prague was the appearance of Charter 77, a human rights manifesto based on the 1975 Final Act of the Conference on Security and Cooperation in Europe (CSCE), and signed, among others, by Vaclav Havel. My job in the Political Section of the U.S. Embassy led me to meet Havel and other Czech dissidents as they were working on the "Charta" as they called it, in the Café Slavia, at Marta Kubišova's farm in East Bohemia, and in other locales. I believe my translation of Charter 77 from Czech into English (typed intentionally out-of-doors on my battery-operated Smith-Corona electric portable to avoid surveillance), was the first such translation of what became a milestone in the fight for human rights in Soviet-dominated Eastern Europe. There was no question but that Western embassies' and journalists' attention to the Czech dissidents' plight was helpful and protective to them in their struggle for greater freedom. The dissidents' notoriety did sometimes land them in jail, as was Havel's fate after signing Charter 77, but silence on our part would have consigned them to complete oblivion. This was a lesson also hammered home by one of my mentors, Ambassador Max Kampelman, whose decision to "name names" – that is, to identify specific Soviet and East European dissidents by name – at the start of the 1980 Madrid Review Conference of the Conference on Security and Cooperation in Europe (CSCE) was controversial at the time, but ultimately helped dissidents struggling for human rights in the U.S.S.R. and elsewhere. The silence of the outside world rarely, if ever, helps the dissident.

I was aware when I employed the word "genocide" that I might well be removed from my ambassadorial position immediately and possibly even drummed out of the Foreign Service, a profession I had loved and in which I had thrived. On my way back to Yerevan, I spent four privately fretful days with my two defense attachés[*] in Stuttgart at a European Command conference for regional chiefs of mission. I was unable to access the Internet from my hotel, and thus incommunicado from my wife, who was still in the United States, and from colleagues who might have some idea what was happening with regard to my "heresy." I reflected on the fact that at least heretics were no longer being burned at the stake, and that I had committed no actual crime. Finally, Deputy Assistant Secretary Laura Kennedy reached me in my Stuttgart hotel room to say that there would be two telegrams on my desk when I arrived in Yerevan; she instructed me to answer both of them before opening of business in Washington on Monday, February 28, which was Assistant Secretary Jones's last day in office. I was relieved to hear that I was free to return to Yerevan – I had truly thought I might be summarily recalled – and took hope and some comfort from the fact that Laura sent her personal regards to Donna.

On my return, there were indeed two cables from the Department on my desk. One was an official reprimand, in the strongest

---

* Lt. Cols. Jeff Predmore and Tripp Jensen.

imaginable terms, from Assistant Secretary Jones. As I was ordered to do, I responded, in terms that were deeply apologetic for my unauthorized action, but resistant on the issue of the historical truth. The second was the text of an Embassy Statement in my name that I was instructed to post to the Embassy website, for all the world to see. The process of posting it was already in progress when I reached my office. But then a most unusual thing occurred: in the process of transcribing the text from a classified telegram and typing it for the unclassified website, the official State Department euphemism "the Armenian tragedy" was altered to read "the Armenian Genocide." I still do not fully understand how this happened. Certainly I did not order it; I was told at the time that it was a "transcription error" on the part of the Armenian staff of our Public Affairs section. The Turkish Ambassador in Washington, Faruk Logoglu, reportedly in the course of "surfing the Web," discovered the use of the offending term, and called Deputy Assistant Secretary Kennedy, who was furious at what appeared to be a further effort – apparently by me – to undermine official policy. Compounding this error – which somehow did *not* occur in the Armenian version of the text – was the fact that our Internet connectivity and telegraphic transmission capability failed precisely on that day, March 1st, and my message to Laura explaining our failure to adhere to the precise wording of the text was delayed in reaching Washington. I was told that my betters at the State Department were "incandescent," but also, intriguingly, that Secretary Rice, newly installed as Secretary of State, had "toned down" the cable excoriating me. I did not know for sure, but wondered whether Dr. Rice's academic sojourn at Stanford might have provided her, like President Reagan, with more understanding of the historical reality of the Armenian Genocide than the rest of my colleagues seemed to possess.

For the remainder of that first week of March, I seriously considered resigning. My upbringing and training inclined me to that option. I ultimately decided not to, partly because my resignation seemed not to have been demanded, except by one member of my staff, who took my "apostasy," as she called it, particularly hard, and, for some unknown reason, very personally. I had not resisted issuing the statement dictated to me by Washington in which I publicly admitted to the world that my speaking out on the issue of the Genocide had been "inappropriate." I had sent apologies privately to Assistant Secretary Jones. I had eaten crow. But there was another reason. It was necessary at this point to open up some space around the issue, to make it easier for my colleagues, and others, to discuss it. To have resigned would only have made it more difficult for others to touch on the issue in the future. It has been rightly said that breaking a taboo has to be punished, if only to prove that the taboo exists and is still in force. As a practical and political matter, the challenge was to sustain a certain level of controversy, while staying on the job. It was admittedly a difficult balancing act. My wife, still in the United States at the time, was greatly comforted and buoyed at this time by Armenian-American friends in Washington, notably Rita and Vartkess Balian and Ross Vartian. Donna gave me good advice: "just keep doing the best possible job you can as Ambassador and hang in there." That was good advice, and that's what I did.

My colleagues were all ears as I opened the first meeting of my Country Team (the Embassy's senior officials) after returning to Yerevan. I explained that, on occasion, in the course of a career in government, one encounters questions of conscience, and that I had just run into one over the issue of the Armenian Genocide. In actual fact, in more than thirty years of U.S. Government service, I had not once encountered a policy issue over which I had felt compelled to fall on my sword. Indeed, I had many times defended U.S. positions with ferocity, as when I argued strenuously and directly with the respected Vaclav Havel, by that time President of Czechoslovakia, over precisely how to characterize President Clinton's visit to Prague.[*] Now, however, I fully expected that there would be serious

---

[*] The White House was insisting that President Clinton was visiting all four of the "Vyšegrad states" and not making a bilateral visit to the Czech Republic. Havel insisted that there was a bilateral component.

consequences for me and my career in the Foreign Service; to begin with, I knew already that I would now no longer be recommended for Presidential Performance Pay.[*] Some members of the Country Team were supportive, but as a group they were divided over my statements regarding the Armenian Genocide. On the one hand, the two highest-ranking members of my State Department staff, the Deputy Chief of Mission and the Political-Economic Counselor, were nearly apoplectic. The latter, borrowing phraseology from Madeleine Albright (on learning of President Clinton's famous peccadillo), announced that she felt "personally betrayed." The DCM fretted that my action would put us out of sync with our British friends, which in fact it did, particularly given that the British Ambassador, a year earlier, had essentially denied that the events of 1915 constituted genocide, thus provoking a diplomatic protest note."[†] On the other hand, several of my colleagues found ways, privately, to let me know they believed that what I had done had been at least morally right. In particular, some of the younger members of the Embassy team told me they supported my efforts, although they dared not let this be known to their immediate supervisors.

The other foreign ambassadors in Yerevan were naturally curious about what had led me so publicly to break with the policy of my own government on the issue of the Armenian Genocide. The Russian Ambassador, Anatoliy Dryukov, was the most unequivocal: he greeted me by pulling me aside and congratulating me for what he called my "civic courage" (*grazhdanskoye muzhestvo*). The French Ambassador, Henry Cuny, a prize-winning novelist in France (under the *nom de plume* Henry Chennevières) was perhaps most fully aware of what an unusual step I had taken; he was quietly but firmly

---

[*] This form of incentive pay for Presidential appointees is more an honor than a major financial benefit. I knew I had been proposed for it because I had seen my draft evaluation report first with my nomination included, then with it excised. Clearly this was done in reaction to my having spoken about the Genocide.

[†] UK Ambassador Thorda Abbott-Watt, in a statement in March, 2004.

Ambassador and Mrs. John Evans, flanked by USAID Director Robin Phillips, to Mrs. Evans's right, DCM Anthony Godfrey, to the Ambassador's left, and other colleagues, paying respects at the Armenian Genocide Memorial in Yerevan, April 24, 2005.

supportive. I privately briefed the British, German, Polish, Italian, Indian and several other ambassadors, making it clear, again, that my own stance did not indicate a change in official U.S. policy on the matter. All save one expressed private sympathy, although publicly they were not prepared to say anything themselves.

Greatly encouraging to me in my embattled situation was the public endorsement of my stance that came unexpectedly from former U.S. Ambassador Harry Gilmore, who had served as our country's first ambassador to Armenia some years earlier. In an interview with Radio Liberty, Harry said, "there is no doubt that the Armenian events were genocide." He went on to say:

> Of course, we have to bear in mind that the Genocide Convention came well after the events in the Ottoman Empire...I think legally there is no question of the Convention applying retroactively. But the key point is that the Convention sets up a standard and the massacres and

deportations of the Ottoman Armenians meet that standard fully…From my thorough study of the events of that period I am persuaded that they do indeed constitute a genocide.[*]

At the same time, figures representing the Executive and Legislative branches also commented. An anonymous "senior official" of the Bush Administration said that my statements "absolutely contradicted" the policy of the U.S. Government. Congressman Frank Pallone, on the other hand, said that "Ambassador Evans simply assigned the word to the definition that was already provided by President Bush as well as members of his administration."[†]

Diplomats do not, as a professional group, like controversy. They are risk-averse to a fault. But controversy is a necessary condition for change. I hoped that the controversy I had stirred up would at least get the issue of the Armenian Genocide out into the open where it could be addressed.

The 90th Anniversary of the Genocide

April 24, 2005 marked the 90th anniversary of the beginning of the 1915 Armenian Genocide, when prominent Armenian intellectuals and other professionals were first rounded up in Constantinople and sent off into exile or eventual annihilation. In what had become a highly anticipated annual event, President George W. Bush issued an official proclamation. It read, in part, as follows:

> This Armenian Remembrance Day marks the 90th anniversary of the forced exile and mass killing of as many as one-and-a-half million Armenians at the end of the Ottoman

---

* Interview with RFE/RL's Emil Danielyan, March 8, 2005.

† Congressman Pallone (D – NJ) is a co-chair of the Congressional Caucus on Armenian Issues.

Empire in what the Armenian people have come to call the "Great Calamity." I express my deepest condolences to the Armenian people on this day of sorrow for all humanity.

This 90th anniversary of these events provides an opportunity for reflection and exploration of historical truth. I hope that the peoples of Turkey and Armenia, and their brethren around the world, can find a way forward to reconcile with their shared past and with each other. This will be a difficult process, steeped in painful memories, especially for those who have personal and community ties to these horrific events.

I applaud recent work of Turks and Armenians who have sought to examine this history of the early 20th Century with honesty and sensitivity. Their results, summed up in an important analysis by the International Center for Transitional Justice, did not provide the final word, but marked a significant step toward reconciliation and restoration of the spirit of tolerance and cultural richness that had connected the people of the Caucasus and Anatolia for centuries. We now look to others to continue this search for a common understanding of the past, aiming to advance a future of freedom, peace and prosperity in Armenia and Turkey in which such horrors never recur. We hope Prime Minster Erdoğan's recent proposal for a joint Turkish-Armenian commission can help advance these processes.[*]

Although the President had used the terms "forced exile" and "mass killing," he had missed the opportunity to call the events "genocide" on the 90th anniversary of their occurrence. I was disappointed, as were many others. Ironically, a few months earlier, I would have been content to see a version of the President's cautious words reflected in the State Department Background Notes.

---

[*] The full text of the statement is available on the White House website: www.whitehouse.gov.

What I understood behind the scenes was that the text was coordinated with top officials at the U.S. Embassy in Ankara, and with the Turkish Ambassador in Washington, but not with the Armenian Ambassador or, for that matter, with me or my staff at the U.S. Embassy in Yerevan. The Turkish Ambassador, as I recall hearing, was not particularly happy with the proclamation's reference to the TARC Study, considering it "one-sided." He was assured by Dan Fried, who received him at the National Security Council, where he was then a Senior Advisor to the President, that at least the statement contained no "incendiary" terms like "genocide" or "ethnic cleansing."[*] Ambassador Logoglu apparently went away somewhat uncomfortable with the statement, but not completely outraged by it. Fried, a former U.S. ambassador to Warsaw, had performed a tricky balancing act; however, the issue was addressed as if it were a purely U.S.-Turkish one, and the consensus of independent historians and experts on the issue was not factored in or acknowledged.

Hrant Dink in Yerevan

To mark the occasion of the 90th anniversary of the Armenian Genocide in April 2005, the Republic of Armenia convened an international conference in Yerevan entitled, "Ultimate Crime and Ultimate Challenge." The Diplomatic Corps – technically, this means all the ambassadors – in Yerevan was invited to attend. Foreign Minister Oskanian personally, in one of his periodic meetings with the resident Ambassadors, urged us all to do so. My staff thought it prudent to ask Washington for permission for me to be present – not to speak, but just to sit in the hall and listen – at the conference. Permission was flatly denied by the State Department. Was it too risky to permit the U.S. Ambassador to *listen in on* the discussion? Was it thought that my presence would lend credence to speculation

---

[*] Almost two years later, on March 15, 2007, Amb. Fried himself used the term "ethnic cleansing," in testimony on U.S.-Turkish relations before the House Foreign Affairs Committee.

that U.S. policy was in flux on the Genocide issue? Or did the State Department simply not want to hear what would be said there?

The conference promised to be an interesting and important one. Genocide scholars from all over the world were on hand. Since I had been explicitly instructed not to attend, my wife Donna, who had been invited in her own right, decided to take up her invitation and demonstratively to sit in the front row. This she did, right next to our good friends the Polish and Italian Ambassadors and their spouses, professional women like my wife. Donna had attended many conferences when she ran the World Affairs Council of Washington; she took copious and good notes, so I obtained, through her, an adequate sense of the proceedings. The Political Section of the U.S. Embassy also dispatched a tag-team of locally engaged employees to record what happened, but, for some reason still not clear to me, the Political Counselor, perhaps with a wink from the Deputy Chief of Mission, deep-sixed the report that might usefully have been sent to Washington. The taboo was, if anything, in fuller effect than ever.

On the evening the conference ended, an unfortunate event took place on the terrace in front of the Armenia Hotel. Several of the conference participants, including the late Turkish-Armenian writer Hrant Dink, the young Turkish scholar Taner Akçam, and the Turkish intellectual and literary critic Murat Belge, were sipping wine in the gathering dusk when a young Armenian man approached their table, asked Prof. Belge if he was a Turk, and, on confirming that he was, splashed red wine in his face.[*] I heard about this in fairly short order through the grapevine, and called Salpi Ghazarian at the Foreign Ministry to inquire about it. Salpi, an Armenian-American, was the Foreign Minister's top aide, and hugely helpful in just such situations, not only to us Americans, but to other embassies as well. Salpi advised me that the young perpetrator was being sought, but that he had raced off and disappeared into the darkness, and was

---

[*] According to an account that appeared in *Hurriyet* on April 25, 2005, Prof. Belge denied that he was asked by his assailant if he was Turkish, and said he had no plans to press charges against the youth.

unlikely to be apprehended. It was an unfortunate display of discourtesy to a visitor.

The next evening, on a hunch, Donna and I went to dine at one of our favorite restaurants, "Dolmama" on Pushkin Street, run by an affable and savvy Armenian-American, Jirair Avanian. As the evening wore on, who should sit down at a neighboring table but Hrant Dink, Murat Belge and Taner Akçam. Although I had been prevented from hearing what these gentlemen, all of them Turkish citizens, had said at the official conference, here was a chance to talk to them in person, informally. I ordered a bottle of red wine and approached their table, introducing myself and offering the wine as solace to Prof. Belge for the unfortunate insult he had suffered at the hands of the wine-pouring Armenian youth. Belge laughed it off and said he was sure he would suffer worse indignities once he was back in Turkey. A fascinating discussion ensued. I came away from it inspired by what these courageous Turks were trying to do against heavy odds: to help their own society come to grips with the historical realities of the Genocide, which remained a taboo subject in Turkey ninety years later. Speaking of the Armenian Genocide is technically punishable under Section 301 of the Turkish penal code. What struck us in particular was Dink's assertion that the vast majority of today's Turkish citizens really do not know the most elementary facts about what happened in 1915. The official history taught in the schools does not deal with it adequately.

Hrant Dink was felled by an assassin's bullet on January 19, 2007, in front of the offices of *Agos*, the Turkish-Armenian newspaper he published. The murder is still being investigated by the Turkish authorities on account of evidence that police in the assassin's home town of Trabzon knew in advance of the young man's intentions. Hrant Dink was a courageous fighter for truth and human dignity. His assassination was a heavy loss for Turks, for Armenians, and for all who strive for proper recognition of the Armenian Genocide and eventual reconciliation between the two nations. He has been included among the ranks of journalists martyred for their

Photocredit : Sebati Karakurt

Hrant Dink

professional activity in the Newseum in Washington. I count it an honor to have met and talked with Hrant Dink, even if I had to do so without the knowledge and permission of the State Department.

The New American Embassy

Since the opening of diplomatic relations with the Republic of Armenia in 1991, the United States had occupied sub-standard official premises. At first, we were located in a suite of rooms in a government-owned hotel-like structure. Later, we purchased the building formerly used by the Communist Youth League (Komsomol) on Baghramian Avenue. It was built of native stone, with a certain dignity and a good downtown location, but our operations were gradually growing, and our security demands were also intensifying in the wake of the 9/11 terrorist attack. It fell to my immediate predecessor as ambassador, John Ordway, to forge an agreement with the relevant Congressional Committees and Washington bureaucrats that co-located the large USAID Mission on grounds to be shared with other elements of the overall US Mission. We purchased a parcel of land abutting Lake Yerevanian on the way to Zvartnots airport, an area of the city that had been inhabited in ancient times, but was currently vacant. At some twenty-two acres, the land was, for the State Department, a large purchase, and the five structures we erected on it were spacious and well-suited to the needs of a middle-sized modern diplomatic mission. The apparent size of the embassy that slowly appeared on the site gave rise to a persistent rumor that the U.S. Government had some nefarious purpose in mind, that the embassy was the largest in the world, or even that there were four hundred marines (or even missiles!) hidden within it. John Ordway explained to me that this misconception must have originated at a press conference he had held to announce the purchase of the land, which was, indeed, a large one for State. Somehow over the years this one fact was spun by local journalists, generally given to conspiracy theories, into a full-blown misconception that the U.S. Embassy was either a "nest of spies" or something other than what it really was: a good design on a fine piece of land, well suited to carrying out the work of a U.S. Mission of medium size, with a robust program of assistance. We had a detachment of five United States Marines led by a Gunnery Sergeant, for a total of six, housed in their own "Marine House." Unlike some modern embassies that resemble fortresses, ours was more like a college campus.

In April, 2005, over the long May-Day weekend, we moved our entire operation from the old building to the new one. It took a tremendous amount of careful planning to pack, label and then move everything, from furniture to files and computers, to the new buildings, but our American and Armenian employees did a fantastic job of it. To cheer morale, a local artist designed a T-shirt for everyone to wear on the big day. At 5:30 on the 28th of April, I lowered the American flag at the old chancery building for the last time. After our successful move, on May 3rd our Marines raised the flag over the new compound, with its splendid view across the lake to Mt. Ararat.

The Constructive Dissent Award

Next there occurred something I couldn't have anticipated. Out of the blue, I was approached by the professional organization of the Foreign Service, the American Foreign Service Association (AFSA), which was considering nominations for, among others, the "Christian A. Herter Award for Constructive Dissent by a Senior Officer." Would I object to being nominated for it? I said I would not. Lo and behold, toward the end of April a telegram from the State Department announced the winners of the 2005 AFSA Awards, and listed me as the recipient of the Herter Award. I received a letter from the President of AFSA congratulating me and stating that "[y]our courageous action in challenging the status quo policy and attempts to promote reconciliation between Turkey and Armenia make you an outstanding candidate for this prestigious award."[*] More than one member of my staff, behind closed doors, shook my hand and congratulated me. DCM Anthony Godfrey said, "You're fire-proofed, boss."

I received dozens of e-mailed messages of congratulations from colleagues in U.S. diplomatic posts all around the world, from the Philippines to Africa.

I felt momentarily vindicated – but the feeling was to be short-lived.

During the month of May, I prepared a comment to be read out on June 17th, on the occasion of my accepting the Herter Award *in absentia*:

---

[*] Letter dated May 12, 2005, from John W. Limbert, then President of AFSA.

By rights, this award should have been given posthumously to the late Ronald Reagan, who used the word "genocide" in his April 22, 1981 Proclamation. I support President Bush's policy of encouraging reconciliation between Turkey and Armenia, as expressed in his latest statement. That statement refers to a legal analysis that found that the word "genocide" was an appropriate description of the events of 1915, but also judged that no claim could be made against any individual or state under the 1948 Genocide Convention. This is a reasonable compromise, ninety years after those events, terrible as they were. I ask that the cash prize accompanying this award be donated directly to the AFSA Scholarship Fund.

My statement never saw the light of day. I never received the Herter Award.

The Herter Award, it turned out, was one nail in my career's coffin. But around this time I committed a further "indiscretion." At a birthday party my wife organized for me in mid-May, Donna spoke openly to our guests about the award that I was to receive in June. In fact, she read aloud from the State Department telegram announcing my receipt of the Herter Award for Constructive Dissent. I responded by recalling dissidents I had known in the past, in Russia and in Czechoslovakia – particularly Vaclav Havel – and thanked our guests for visiting a diplomat who now knew what it was like to be considered a dissident by his own government. Somehow details of that birthday dinner seem to have gotten back to Washington, the story line being that "the Ambassador is unrepentant." Indeed I was *privately* unrepentant, although I had pledged not to raise the Genocide issue again *in public* while Ambassador. In fact, I had never addressed it while at my duty station in Armenia, only in America. I considered the matter to be a moral and political issue *in the United States*, and treated it as such. On occasion, when Armenians approached me to thank me for what I had said, I told them they had no need to thank me, that I had said what I said for the sake of my own country: the United States of America. Whether my birthday party was a private or a public event is a close call. Given that foreign officials were present, I have to confess it had a semi-public nature and may have given rise to persistent press reports that I was removed for having used the word "genocide" in a "social setting."

At the beginning of June, I was summoned urgently to Washington by the new Assistant Secretary of State for European and Eurasian Affairs, Dan Fried, a former friend and colleague with whom I had worked on the Soviet Desk, who had recently moved from the National Security Council to the State Department. He wanted me to come immediately, but I had to delay my departure by a day to see through the visit of Senator Norm Coleman (R – Minnesota). I had asked to have some time alone with Dan, but instead, when I reached his office directly from the airport after a sixteen-hour flight, I was faced with what clearly was a hanging court, complete with a representative of the Director General of the Foreign Service (Bob Pearson, a former ambassador to Ankara) and the Executive Director of the European Bureau. For the next forty minutes, Assistant Secretary Fried gave me a tongue-lashing, most painfully accusing me of wanting to "jam" the President, which I vehemently denied, pointing out that I had based my remarks, which I had characterized as my personal view, on the ICTJ study that the President's own proclamation praised. I hardly had a chance to make my case, although Fried claimed he had read – and dismissed – an e-mailed explanation of my views. Dan demanded to know whether I had rejected the AFSA Award. I responded truthfully: that I had "not declined" it. This put me in an awkward position. It was clear that the AFSA Award had raised the temperature around the matter, and that the Department could not abide the thought that I would receive it (albeit *in absentia*) in the Ben Franklin Room on June 17. Turkish Prime Minister Erdoğan was due in Washington within days, which probably heightened the stakes for the State Department. At the strong suggestion of the "hanging court," I contacted AFSA to explain the situation. The Herter Award was withdrawn on a technicality, namely, that I had not registered my dissent from policy via the Dissent Channel.[*] The Herter Award was not conferred on anyone that year. It was left undecided at that point what further punishment would be meted out, but I gathered that another shoe would drop.

And one did. On July 2, while having dinner with friends, including Deputy Foreign Minister Arman Kirakossian and his lovely wife Susanna at "The Club", a subterranean Yerevan restaurant, I received a call on my cell phone from Dan Fried. I went up to street level to take it. Dan relayed the State Department's verdict: I would, for my "sin" of having used the word "genocide," be removed from my post a year earlier than anticipated, in 2006. There would be no announcement; my job would simply be listed as a "2006 vacancy." I told Dan that, in that case, it was my intention to retire, as I would by then have been in the Foreign Service for thirty-five years and it was clearly time for me and the State Department to part ways. I returned to the dinner party and did not let on that anything unusual had happened. My wife Donna asked if everything was alright. I indicated that it was. When we got home that evening I broke the news to her as we sat on our favorite upstairs porch: we would be leaving Yerevan a year early, and I would "retire" ahead of my expected date. It was a tough moment for us both as we sat overlooking the lights of Yerevan. I was resigned to taking the punishment that my actions had precipitated. But Donna was furious. She was just then preparing to return to New York to help our daughter, at this point in the throes of her divorce, but before she left, she sat down at her laptop and wrote a letter directly to First Lady Laura Bush that she FedExed to the White House on arrival. I did not see the text of the letter, and could only guess what Donna might have written. It was never answered or acknowledged.

As it turned out, I remained at my post for an additional fourteen months. Although I had crossed the State Department on a

---

* The Washington *Post* ran a story about my loss of the award in its June 9, 2005 edition, just below a photograph of Prime Minister Erdoğan at the White House with President Bush.

particularly sensitive issue, no one could credibly claim that I was not
otherwise doing an excellent job, supported by an extraordinarily fine
Mission (Embassy) team. I continued to carry out the full range of
activities expected of any ambassador, opening exhibits, traveling to
parts of the Republic of Armenia where U.S. assistance programs –
especially the Peace Corps, our favorite – were active, and meeting
and briefing visitors. If anything, knowing privately that my tour was
to be prematurely curtailed, I threw myself into my work with extra
vigor and enthusiasm. Most significantly, I put the Embassy firmly
on record as supporting the rapid evolution of Armenia toward
democracy, but not revolution in the streets, as some Armenian
politicians – notably Aram Z. Sargsian of the Republic Party – were
then advocating. This I did most comprehensively in a speech at the
American University in Armenia entitled "The Continuing Effect of
the American Revolution." It was a tribute in part to the late British
historian Arnold Toynbee, who had given a talk in Williamsburg
forty years earlier on that topic. The State Department liked my
speech, and distributed the text worldwide via USINFO.[*] I got
enthusiastic feedback from as far away as Beijing. Locally, the
Yerevan media (*Haikakan Jamanak* in particular) were suspicious:
how could the American Ambassador, who had taken a position at
variance with U.S. policy on the Genocide, at the same time have his
speech about building democracy approved and then circulated by
the State Department?

  As for my own impending fate, no one besides me and my wife
knew, after Dan Fried's call, what had now been set in motion. The
first person outside the Embassy circle to detect that something was
up was Arpi Vartanian, the clever Yerevan-based representative of the
Armenian Assembly of America. Arpi called me in late July, 2005,
and asked if I was aware that my position had been listed by the State
Department as a "vacancy" in the summer of 2006. I complimented
her on having "good sources," but said that there would be no official

---

[*] The State Department's electronic distribution system for public affairs
materials.

announcement about the matter, and that I had nothing to say. My wife and I were about to leave for a vacation in France beginning with a week at the Normandy farmstead of my old friend Michael Lemmon and his French wife Michele. Just before leaving, I gave my deputy, Anthony Godfrey, a sealed envelope containing suggested press guidance in case the story of my impending early departure broke during August. In the event, it did not, but Anthony was now alerted to the possibility that he might end up serving as Chargé d'Affaires for a longer period than that of my vacation, which ultimately he did, filling out what would normally have been my third year as Ambassador.

Howard Dean Visits Yerevan

At summer's end, who should visit Armenia but Howard Dean, Chairman of the Democratic National Committee. Governor Dean had been a student at Yale at the same time as I, but we had not really known each other in those days. Despite the political risk to me, as President Bush's envoy, of hosting a major player in the "Democrat Party," we gave Dean a full briefing, including a session with the entire Country Team. As we were wrapping it up with a photographic session in front of our new Chancery (the main embassy office building), Dean off-handedly asked me where I would be assigned next. I told him that my Foreign Service career was at an end on account of what I had said about the Armenian Genocide. He was shocked and expressed dismay, saying he thought it was unfair on the part of the State Department. I did not know it at the time, but one member of the Embassy staff, Tressa Finerty, our capable Cultural Affairs officer, overheard this exchange; she later asked questions of, and was sworn to secrecy by, the DCM. None of us on the Embassy staff who knew I would be leaving early wanted to weaken our position – to make a lame duck out of me – prematurely. But from this time on, it became clear to me that more and more people seemed to know. The word was slowly getting out.

Governor Dean was visiting Armenia as a guest of the Armenian National Committee of America, which is politically close to the Armenian Revolutionary Federation, or Dashnaks. He appeared at a ceremony in a new Yerevan hotel after his visit to the Embassy. In his remarks, heard by several key members of my own staff, as well as by Armenians, he spoke sincerely and movingly about the importance of basing policy on the truth. He came out clearly in favor of recognition of the Armenian Genocide for what it was. What we saw was that he was a fine speaker and not limited to "the scream" as purveyed on You Tube. We posted a story about Dean's visit to the Embassy website, and I never heard a word of complaint from the State Department or the White House about his visit – as I had frankly feared we might.

Recall

Eventually, just before Christmas in 2005, we got wind of the fact that the President intended to nominate Richard E. Hoagland, an acquaintance of mine from the State Department when we each had headed a Country Desk, to succeed me as Ambassador in Yerevan. The choice made sense: Hoagland had served as Director of the Office of Central Asia and the Caucasus. He had then become Ambassador to Tajikistan. He knew the area well. From the point of view of the State Department, he could be counted on to adhere strictly to policy on, among other things, the Armenian Genocide. Hoagland was present at a conference of American Ambassadors assigned to Europe and Eurasia that was held at the State Department in early January. I recall his first words to me at a reception where, each of us knowing about the plans for him to replace me, we connected: he said firmly, "I *always* do as I am told." I took that not only as a reproach for my own "disobedience" but also as a signal that Dick would toe the reigning policy line unquestioningly. Fair enough: that was to be expected.

A few weeks later, a telegram arrived for my "eyes only." It was an instruction to seek the *agrément* of the President of the Republic of Armenia to the appointment of Dick Hoagland as ambassador. I arranged to meet with President Kocharian solo, without even a note-taker present. I thought it was important to explain to Kocharian honestly why I was leaving a year earlier than anticipated. Only my secretary, the loyal and discreet Pauline Maurantonio, knew of these arrangements. President Kocharian understood the situation clearly. We had a very solid relationship, based on candid discussions while listening to jazz in Yerevan's excellent jazz clubs, most memorably Chez Malkhas. I especially valued his willingness to be frank about problems, but also his keen sense of humor. Given Armenia's growing pains as a young democracy, I am sure Kocharian was not always happy to hear what I had to convey in our many meetings, but our relations were proper and open. Now, on the difficult matter of my own impending departure, Kocharian showed appropriate sympathy. I had the impression he was in no hurry to give his assent, as requested, to the appointment of a new U.S. ambassador. The question had, in any case, to await the return to Yerevan and action of the Foreign Minister, Vartan Oskanian. The State Department had asked for prompt verbal confirmation that the Government of Armenia had no objection to the appointment. State clearly wanted me out of Yerevan sooner rather than later. But it turned out to be not quite that simple. The controversy over the issue continued raging in the Armenian and especially in the Diasporan press, and was about to reach a high point in the spring of 2006 in connection with our departure.

Yellow Ribbons

The April 24, 2006 anniversary of the start of the 1915 Genocide was approaching when word of Hoagland's impending nomination[*] and my early departure leaked out. The most perceptive observer of the drama was Harut Sassounian, publisher of the California *Courier*, a weekly newspaper for Armenian-Americans. Through a combination of excellent contacts in Yerevan and plain hard journalistic work,

[*] Dick's nomination was officially announced by the White House on May 23, 2006.

The Armenian graphic artist "Patrik" captured the moment in this sketch.

Harut somehow managed to piece together the various bits of information and tell his readers, almost in real time, what was going on. So accurate was Harut in his weekly column, printed with a slight delay in Armenia, that some observers may have imagined I was briefing him on the sly. That was not, in fact, the case.

The local reaction to my recall among Armenian-Americans living in Yerevan was what surprised me. These are the so-called "re-pats" – Armenians who have repatriated themselves to their ancestral homeland – who are living and working in the Republic of Armenia, primarily in the professions. Somehow they coalesced around the charismatic figure of Edith Khachaturian, the young lawyer from San Francisco, and launched the "Yellow Ribbon Campaign" to support me – as fellow American citizens resident in Armenia – and to object to my being recalled. As a slogan, Edith chose the words of Dr. Martin Luther King, Jr.: "In the end we will remember not the words of our enemies, but the silence of our friends." This sentence captured the essence of what many Armenian-Americans, young and old, feel about their own government's failure adequately to recognize the Armenian Genocide for what it was. Edith and her friends had Dr. King's words, in English and Armenian, emblazoned on a T-shirt that also bore a poignant image of the Yerevan Genocide Memorial surrounded by barbed wire. They had posters designed and printed on the same theme. All of this was done with minimal financial resources, and largely by local people. That the campaign was centered on supporting me and pressing Washington not to recall me was, in a sense, incidental; it had more to do with the fact that I had become a symbol to Armenians of something they yearned for: an American diplomat who would acknowledge the truth about 1915. At the same time, I did feel that some proportion of the popular support for my continuing in office was based on the very positive interactions I had had with many Armenians, particularly young ones, in the short time I had been ambassador.

On the evening of April 24, when, by tradition, Armenians of all descriptions, the high clergy, the President and his Ministers, the military brass and schoolchildren in their thousands file past the Genocide Memorial atop Tsitsernakaberd Hill and pay homage to the victims of the Young Turks, the organizers of the Yellow Ribbon Campaign stood vigil on the path approaching the cavernous monument. They passed out yellow ribbons and encouraged the thousands of pilgrims passing by to tie them to a series of horizontal wires strung along their path. During the night and continuing into the morning, the wires grew heavy with the yellow ribbons, until there was a veritable wall of yellow. Architect Eduard Balassanian, one of the conspirators, explained to a TV interviewer what the yellow ribbon symbolized for Americans: "In America we hang out yellow ribbons when someone has been taken hostage, but in this case, *it is the truth that has been taken hostage.*"

One of the inconsistencies of U.S. policy on the question of the Armenian Genocide is that the American Ambassador in Yerevan *is* authorized to participate in the official wreath-laying that the local Diplomatic Corps carries out on April 24 at Yerevan's hilltop Genocide Memorial, despite the general U.S. policy of not recognizing the Genocide. Harry Gilmore was the first U.S. Ambassador to lay a wreath, and every one since then has done so. U.S. Ambassadors in other capitals, for example, in France, are not authorized to participate in local Armenian remembrance events. Furthermore, the Ambassador in Yerevan is permitted to take members of his Country Team with him on this ceremonial occasion, although he is on strict instructions not to speak. In both of the years I led the American Embassy contingent, there was no lack of interest on the part of my staff, and April 24, 2006 was no exception: all members of the Country Team were present on that rainy, overcast morning. But a little surprise awaited us. Right before the entrance to the eternal flame that burns in the central sunken area of the Memorial, a chorus of young Armenians carrying fistfuls of yellow ribbons was on hand to thank me for having broken silence on the question of the Genocide.

It was in some ways an awkward moment, fraught with the possibility of sending wrong signals, or no signal. I acknowledged the young people in the best way I could, placing my hand on my heart and bowing slightly in their direction. Other members of the Embassy team were either unaware of or unaffected by the show of local solidarity. The French Ambassador discreetly wore a yellow necktie to signal his own *solidarité*.[*]

After laying our wreath, which bore a ribbon with written condolences from the staff of the Embassy, but not from the American people as a whole,[†] we stood silently for a moment in the rain, my wife beside me looking uncharacteristically somber. As we made our way back to the plaza surrounding the Memorial, we ran directly into a solid phalanx of radio and TV reporters. I was under strict instructions not to "open my mouth," but the moment demanded I

---

[*] Alex Sardar, a "repat" to Armenia from San Francisco, informed us that yellow ribbons appeared again, spontaneously, on the 92nd commemoration of the Genocide in Yerevan on April 24, 2007.

[†] This formulation is an awkward signal that the observance is sanctioned only locally, not world-wide.

The 2006 Genocide commemoration at the Tsitsernakaberd.

The 2006 Genocide commemoration at the Tsitsernakaberd.

The 2006 Genocide commemoration at the Tsitsernakaberd.

say something appropriate to the occasion. So I looked directly at the cameras and clearly and sincerely pronounced "God bless you!" Then I walked back toward my car, where my driver was patiently waiting for us. Whether it was reported to Washington that I had technically violated my instructions by "opening my mouth," I did not very much care at that point. I was told that some Armenian television viewers, on hearing my impromptu remark, had burst into tears.[*]

Resignation

The White House formally announced that the President had nominated career Foreign Service Officer Richard Eugene Hoagland as my successor on May 23, 2006. This was my cue to resign, and I did so in a letter to President Bush dated May 30 that contained the required formula, "I hereby tender my resignation as Ambassador to the Republic of Armenia, to become effective at your pleasure." It went on to state:

---

[*] Edith Khachaturian.

When, over a year ago, I spoke openly at Berkeley and U.C.L.A. about the tragedy that befell the Armenians of the Ottoman Empire in 1915, I did not do so with any intent to flout your authority on this or any other matter; rather, after examining the historical record and the relevant legal texts, I had reached a crisis of conscience that I was unable to resolve other than by speaking my mind, while making it clear that my own view of the issue differed from official policy.

I then thanked the President for the privilege of serving our country.

In August I received a short, but cordial note from President Bush thanking me for my service and wishing me and my family well. But by that time the nomination of Mr. Hoagland had run into difficulty in the Senate Foreign Relations Committee (SFRC) over the double question of why I was being recalled and whether Dick had slipped back from official policy by responding to a question about the Armenian Genocide through use of the word "alleged" or "allegations." It was not my business to become in any way involved with the confirmation of my successor. I therefore refrained entirely from doing so. When Dick's confirmation was unexpectedly held up until after the August recess, I communicated to Dan Fried my willingness to stay in place until such time as the Senate acted on the nomination. I received an instruction back from Dan to "depart post by the end of the first week in September." Consideration of Dick Hoagland's nomination had been rescheduled for September 7. It seemed obvious to me that the State Department wanted to be able to argue that Embassy Yerevan lacked an ambassador. Because of an early Labor Day and a sailing mishap on Lake Sevan in which I nearly cracked my skull,* Donna and I were not able to depart until

---

* I tumbled into the bilges of a catamaran while sailing through a blow on Lake Sevan, an incident that immediately became known as "Ambassador down the hatch." I could have broken my neck, but got first aid from Diana Melkoumian, an Armenian doctor on board, and then superb stitches from our capable health practitioner, Paul McOmber. Paul pulled my stitches out less than 24 hours before our flight home.

September 10. In the event, Senator Bob Menendez (D – New Jersey) placed a "hold" on Dick's nomination. The SFRC was evenly divided over the issue, with some Republicans as well as Democrats opposing the nomination. It was Senator Menendez's hold that stopped the nomination from going forward, but I understand there were three or four other Senators who had communicated to Armenian-American organizations their willingness to place a hold if Menendez withdrew his. As it turned out, Senator Menendez won his tight election battle in New Jersey and promptly renewed the hold when Dick's nomination was resubmitted to the Senate in January 2007. The nomination was never approved, and Hoagland eventually asked President Bush to withdraw his name from consideration in July 2007.[*]

A year and a half after the controversy over my departure and Dick Hoagland's nomination in the Senate Foreign Relations Committee, I became aware of what one member of that Committee had said in a letter to Secretary of State Rice. The Senator wrote: "…I believe that the controversy over Ambassador Evans' use of the term 'genocide' underscores the fact that the current U.S. position is untenable. That the invocation of a historical fact by a State Department employee could constitute an act of insubordination is deeply troubling. When State Department instructions are such that an ambassador must engage in strained reasoning – or even an outright falsehood – that defies a common sense interpretation of events in order to follow orders, then it is time to revisit the State Department's policy guidance on that issue. The occurrence of the Armenian genocide in 1915 is not an 'allegation,' a 'personal opinion,' or a 'point of view.' Supported by an overwhelming amount of historical evidence, it is a widely documented fact." The Senator went on to cite examples of the evidence and concluded, "[w]hile I believe that neither the Department of State nor U.S. Congress should be attempting to

---

[*] Marie Louise Yovanovitch was nominated to the post by President Bush on March 31, 2008 and confirmed by the Senate on August 1.

write the history of 1915, the U.S. Government should endeavor to align its policies with facts that have been well-established by credible historians."*

Regrets?

Do I have any regrets? Yes. I do regret the dissatisfaction – indeed anger – that my candor on the subject of the Armenian Genocide caused my colleagues at the State Department, who are not evil people but are simply trying to conduct the Nation's business as best they can. I also regret the reactions of some of my former Turkish colleagues and friends, who took my honesty on the historical issue of the Genocide almost as a personal affront. At the same time, I do not regret that, having researched the issue and considered it carefully, I had leveled with my audiences in Massachusetts and California about both the historical facts, the appropriateness of the term "genocide" to describe them, and current international political realities. *The taboo had to be broken. The truth had to be told.* And as William Penn famously said, "[S]omebody must begin it." I was speaking to fellow American citizens, "hyphenated Americans," perhaps (and who in America isn't?) but loyal tax-paying citizens of our land who for too long have felt that their own government has given them a callous and deceptive brush-off on an issue of supreme importance to them. Ultimately, all Americans who serve in the Federal Government owe their allegiance and their honesty first of all to the citizens of this country. I swore allegiance to the Constitution, not to a particular leader, and not to a policy that I could not in good conscience support. It is true that the President decides foreign policy; however, the Armenian Genocide was not a "normal" foreign policy issue: it seemed to me to warrant unusual action on my part. I was not

---

* Letter from Senator Barack Obama to Secretary of State Rice dated July 28, 2006.

On Lake Sevan.

content to fall back on the Nuremberg (and Eichmann) defense that I was "just following orders."

What can be said for sure is that it is time for our friends and allies the modern-day Turks to reexamine what some – not all – of their forebears did to the indigenous Armenian (as well as Greek and Assyrian) minority Christian populations of the declining Ottoman Empire in 1915-16. The precise numbers of victims can be debated, as can the circumstances leading to the massacres, but there is no doubt but that it was a genocide. More and more well-informed Turks actually know and at least privately admit this. The Genocide Convention does not specify a magic number at which point the crime rises to the level of "genocide." Nor does it require that every member of the targeted group be destroyed. And it does not require that a duly constituted governing authority, such as a sitting cabinet of ministers, officially undertake, in writing, the destruction of a people. No single written order by Hitler for the destruction of the European Jews has ever been located, but no sane person today denies the reality of the Holocaust. These points are often lost sight of in the heat of argument, but that does not alter the central truth.

To their credit, some courageous Turks are now bravely attempting to wrestle with this painful issue. Hrant Dink, a Turkish citizen of Armenian descent, was one of them. Nobel Laureate Orhan Pamuk is another. Novelist Elif Shafak is yet another. The publisher Ragip Zarakolu, recently convicted under Section 301 of the Turkish Penal Code of "insulting the Turkish Nation" for having published a translation of George Jerjian's book *The Truth Will Set Us Free,** is another. And historian Taner Akçam is courageously publishing original research to prove that the official version of history is deceptive. All of these brave Turks have run into difficulties with the Turkish authorities on account of their views. Eventually, it will become evident that, in addition to those who wanted to obliterate the Armenians and create an "Anatolia for the Turks," there were also individuals of conscience – some call them "righteous" Turks – who did not support the genocidal policies of the Young Turk regime. Taner Akçam has dedicated a book to one of these "righteous Turks," Haji Halil, a devout Muslim who harbored Armenians at a time when to do so was a criminal action.† As for the Armenians, both in the far-flung Diaspora, where the issue of the Genocide tends to dominate the agenda, and in the Republic of Armenia, where it is on the agenda but does not top the list, the time may have come to reconsider the more far-reaching and aggressive claims that some have advanced, understandably but impracticably, against Turkey. For the future of the region, both sides need to step back from the most extreme positions, which feed on each other, and work to establish diplomatic relations, open the closed border, and consolidate economic and trade relations that will benefit present and future

---

* George Jerjian, *The Truth Will Set Us Free: Armenians and Turks Reconciled.* (London: GJ Publications, 2003), with a Foreword by former U.S. Senator Bob Dole.

† Taner Akçam, *A Shameful Act: The Armenian Genocide and the Question of Turkish Responsibility.* New York: Metropolitan Books, 2006.

generations. A joint historical commission, so long as it is not used to delay these urgent goals and so long as it does not cast doubt on the central historical fact of the matter, is not necessarily a bad idea. It should include a credible third party who can referee the process and prevent it from being a sterile exchange of vituperative monologues. There does need to be some sort of sincere apology by the Turkish authorities, followed by a serious effort on their part to make at least partial amends. Otherwise, a great crime will have taken place and gone both unpunished – the original perpetrators, of course, are now beyond the reach of any punishment – and unavowed. Strictly legal or criminal "justice" is elusive in a case like this, but a serious offer of *at least a measure* of moral and material compensation needs to be made in memory of the victims, and on behalf of their descendants.

Part II
The Armenian Genocide...

Was it Really a Case of Genocide?

Yes, it was: the "ayes" have it by a long shot. It recently came to light that the U.S. Government, in a legal filing at the International Court of Justice in The Hague in 1951, had the following to say about the 1915 massacres:

> The Genocide Convention resulted from the inhuman and barbarous practices which prevailed in certain countries prior to and during World War II, when entire religious, racial and national minority groups were threatened with and subjected to deliberate extermination. The practice of genocide has occurred throughout human history. The Roman persecution of the Christians, the *Turkish massacres of Armenians*, the extermination of millions of Jews and Poles by the Nazis are *outstanding examples of the crime of genocide.*[*]
> (emphasis added)

1951 was a year before Turkey became a member of the NATO Alliance and before Armenians world-wide had begun their campaign for Genocide recognition. But this laconic and straightforward statement remains on the books as a challenge to latter-day, policy-driven attempts to deny or distort the truth and withhold the accurate term, which is "genocide."

This is not to say that there is no room for controversy about certain aspects of the question, as Turkish government spokesmen and historians and a handful of Western historians vehemently insist. One of the bitter ironies surrounding the complex tragedy of 1915-16 is that Armenian families *know* from their own parents and grandparents, surviving great-uncles and aunts, and other relatives, what happened to their own kin, and yet there is precious little definitive "proof" of the sort that might suffice to prevail in a court of law. Historians debate whether this is because original Ottoman

---

* Written Statement of the Government of the United States, Advisory Opinion of May 28th, 1951, p. 23.

INTERNATIONAL COURT OF JUSTICE

PLEADINGS, ORAL ARGUMENTS, DOCUMENTS

RESERVATIONS TO THE
CONVENTION ON THE PREVENTION
AND PUNISHMENT OF THE
CRIME OF GENOCIDE

ADVISORY OPINION OF MAY 28th, 1951

CONTENTS
SECTION C.—WRITTEN STATEMENTS

4. WRITTEN STATEMENT OF THE GOVERNMENT OF THE
UNITED STATES OF AMERICA

WRITTEN STATEMENT OF THE U.S.A. 25

I. *The Genocide Convention*

The Genocide Convention resulted from the inhuman and barbarous practices which prevailed in certain countries prior to and during World War II, when entire religious, racial and national minority groups were threatened with and subjected to deliberate extermination. The practice of genocide has occurred throughout human history. The Roman persecution of the Christians, the Turkish massacres of Armenians, the extermination of millions of Jews and Poles by the Nazis are outstanding examples of the crime of genocide. This was the background when the General Assembly of the United Nations considered the problem of genocide. Not once, but twice, that body declared unanimously that the practice of genocide is criminal under international law and that States ought to take steps to prevent and punish genocide.

official records have been lost or intentionally destroyed, or because the orders to exterminate the Armenian population were conveyed through special secret channels, or for some other reason. This debate is among one of the most fascinating, and harrowing, of the entire historical period. It is not merely about whether orders were issued, which is relevant to the larger question of whether there was "intent" to commit genocide. It also involves the question of the Armenian properties that were seized by the Ottoman state and parceled out to Turkish expellees from the lost Ottoman lands in the Balkans and to Muslims who would become the backbone of the Turkish middle class. The children and infants who survived the deportations and massacres carried with them no deeds to their family homes; they had the awful experiences seared into their memories, but many did not even know their own names or remember their parents' faces when they emerged from the chaos and terror of it all. Sadly, as Taner Akçam has shown, Turkish official records about the Armenians' confiscated properties are more complete than the records of what happened to the people.[*]

The first milestone on my journey of inquiry into the question of the Armenian Genocide was the remarkable book by Ambassador Henry Morgenthau, President Woodrow Wilson's envoy to the Ottoman Empire 1913-16, *Ambassador Morgenthau's Story*. As the representative of a neutral power, with a network of consuls in the field who sent him information, as did the large number of American missionaries, Morgenthau was unusually well informed. He also enjoyed remarkable access to a number of the crucial participants in the events, most notably Talaat Pasha, the Minister of the Interior at the time. Morgenthau met repeatedly with Talaat during the period of the deportations, and was himself also an actor in the drama, vainly imploring Washington to authorize him to intervene in some way to mitigate the awful events that were underway. The chapter

---

[*] Taner Akçam, "Deportation and Massacres in the Cipher Telegrams of the Interior Ministry in the Prime Ministerial Archive (Başbakanlık Arşivi)" *Genocide Studies and Prevention*, 1(3) Winter 2006, p. 316.

titles from Morgenthau's book that bear most directly on the
Armenian Genocide are in themselves revealing: "The Murder of a
Nation," "Talaat Tells Why He 'Deports' the Armenians," "Enver
Pasha Discusses the Armenians," and "I Shall do Nothing for the
Armenians' Says the German Ambassador."[*] Some critics have
attacked Ambassador Morgenthau's book, which was published a few
years after the events, in 1918, and pointed out that there are
discrepancies between the book and his private diaries. This may
indeed be the case – I have not myself reviewed the Diaries – but I do
not believe it in any major way vitiates the overall conclusion that the
reader takes away from his public account.[†] After all, Morgenthau
concludes by saying that the events constituted "the annihilation of
the Armenian race."[‡] Elsewhere he writes of the "destruction of the
Armenians,"[**] and sums up the events up as "race murder." It could
not have been put any more clearly than this – until Raphael Lemkin
coined the virtually synonymous term, "genocide," in 1944.

A second category of source materials, other diplomatic accounts,
has been thoroughly mined for materials bearing on the question of
whether there was "intent" to exterminate the Armenians of Anatolia.
Within this category, the accounts of foreign diplomats representing
the Central Powers, notably the German and Austrian diplomats and
military officers, are especially useful. Vahakn Dadrian's *German
Responsibility in the Armenian Genocide: A Review of the Historical
Evidence of German Complicity*[††] relies heavily on these sources,
which are still being studied. More recently, materials in the papers of
the lone Danish representative to the Sublime Porte, Carl Ellis
Wandel, who served in Constantinople 1914-25, have come to

---

[*] These are chapters XXIV – XXVII in Morgenthau's account.

[†] Thomas G. Leonard deals with the issue of Morgenthau's diaries in note
16 of his article "When News is not Enough: American Media and
Armenian Deaths," in Winter, op. cit., pp. 302-03.

[‡] Morgenthau, op. cit., p. 273.

[**] Ibid., p. 321.

[††] Vahakn Dadrian, Cambridge, MA: Blue Crane Books, 1996.

light.[*] Wandel reported to the Danish Foreign Ministry in Copenhagen that "[t]he Turks are vigorously carrying out their cruel intent, to exterminate the Armenian people."[†]

Although the diplomatic dispatches and official materials of the Allied Powers in World War I, starting with the magisterial treatment of the events by Arnold Toynbee in the British "Blue Book",[‡] are sometimes scorned by Turkish historians as "war propaganda," the truth is that they contain many facts and judgments by professionals whose honesty and discernment we ought to trust. But, as Donald Bloxham, a young British scholar, has shown in his *Great Game of Genocide*,[**] the Allied Powers, especially Great Britain and Russia, were far from blameless in their maneuvering for position, exploitation of the Armenians for geopolitical gain, and designs against the Turkish state in its final years of decline. There were many ingredients in the Armenian Genocide, and there is responsibility enough to be spread widely around. Even the Armenians themselves were not totally blameless: some of them not only harbored "seditious" thoughts, but acted on them, rose up in some places, hoping that the war would precipitate a collapse of the hated Empire, and, in some instances, killed Turks and Kurds. Most of these instances, much remarked upon by partisans of the Turkish version of history, were revenge killings or acts of self-defense, but they did happen, and Armenian historians ought not to fear acknowledging them. In their totality, of course, these isolated acts of violence

---

* Matthias Bjornlund, "'When the Cannons Talk, the Diplomats Must be Silent': A Danish Diplomat in Constantinople during the Armenian Genocide" *Genocide Studies and Prevention*, Vol. 1, No. 2, Fall 2006.

† Ibid., p. 210.

‡ Great Britain, Parliament of. *The Treatment of Armenians in the Ottoman Empire: Documents Presented to Viscount Grey of Fallodon, Secretary of State for Foreign Affairs,* (1916). Reprinted Astoria: NY:J.C. and A.L. Fawcett, 1990. Also critical edition Gomidas Institute, 2nd ed., 2005.

** Donald Bloxham, *The Great Game of Genocide: Imperialism, Nationalism and the Destruction of the Ottoman Armenians.* New York: Oxford University Press, 2005.

perpetrated by Armenians, many of them in the course of fighting on the Russian-Turkish front in 1918, do not in any way condone what was done to Armenian women, children and old people, and to unarmed Armenian men.

Turkish apologists sometimes lament that the archives of the Dashnak (or Tashnag) Party, the Armenian Revolutionary Federation (ARF), have not been opened for general inspection. The main archives of the Dashnaks, one of the historic Armenian political parties, founded in Tbilisi in 1890, are located in Boston. In actual fact, the ARF archives have been catalogued and opened up as far as the year 1925, according to the archivist who was in charge of them until 2000, Tatul Sonentz-Papazian.[*] They probably could profit from additional examination by independent scholars, but my guess is that, since they have mostly to do with intrigues in the Caucasus and fighting on the Eastern (Russian-Turkish) front, they will not yield much to mitigate the responsibility of the Ottoman authorities – or at least of the Young Turks – in the matter of the Genocide in Anatolia. They could yield accounts of revenge atrocities that might make for discomfort in some quarters, but are unlikely to alter the fundamental facts.

Another source of eye-witness evidence to the Armenian Genocide are the statements of American missionaries who were active in the Ottoman Empire during the period leading up to the First World War. In 1917 the Reverend James Barton, head of the American Board of Commissioners for Foreign Missions, solicited formal statements from American missionaries who had completed their missions in Anatolia. The results, divided into first-hand observations and second-hand, but reliable, hearsay, make for horrifying reading.[†]

---

[*] As quoted in Asbarez.com, May 23, 2008. Sonentz-Papazian went on to say that Turkish scholars were welcome to study the archives and that several Armenian scholars had already done so.

[†] James L. Barton, *"Turkish Atrocities": Statements of American Missionaries on the Destruction of Christian Communities in Ottoman Turkey, 1915-1917.* Ann Arbor, MI: Gomidas Institute, 1998.

On the controversial issue of the Armenian rebellion at Van, it is worth reading Clarence Ussher's first-hand account, in which he makes clear that the Armenians demonstrated "patience under almost unimaginable provocation."[*]

The Ottoman Archives are voluminous and working in them is greatly complicated by the fact that the records are in Ottoman Turkish, using a version of the Persian script that was scrapped by Atatürk in the Alphabet Reform of 1928. Even many Turkish scholars cannot easily work with them. In addition, free access to these archives by "suspect" foreign scholars has apparently been limited by the Turkish authorities. Taner Akçam, the Turkish historian, who has worked in several of the available archives, reports that "working conditions in the Ottoman archives have been an issue in the past. Problems included difficulty in obtaining catalogs, the arbitrary rejection of requests to photocopy documents, the dismissal of 'suspicious' people from the archives, and the theft of research materials from visitors." Akçam also points out that no one has had full access to the documents. But his conclusion is that "...we need to reassess the idea that Ottoman archival materials contradict Western archival materials. They are not mutually exclusive; on the contrary, they are in compliance with each other."[†]

Hitherto unknown materials are constantly coming to the surface. Perhaps the most notable recent find was the so-called "Black Book" compiled by Talaat Pasha, preserved by his widow and published by a Turkish journalist in 2009. [‡] There is also movement in official

---

[*] Clarence D. Ussher, *An American Physician in Turkey: A Narrative of Adventures in Peace and War*. Originally published by Houghton Mifflin: Boston and New York, 1917, now available in a facsimile edition published by J. C. and A. L. Fawcett: Woodside, NY, 1990.

[†] Taner Akçam, "Deportation and Massacres in the Cipher Telegrams of the Interior Ministry in the Prime Ministerial Archive (Başbakanlık Arşivi)" in *Genocide Studies and Prevention*, Volume 1, No. 3, Winter 2006, p. 306.

[‡] Sabrina Tavernise, "Nearly a Million Genocide Victims, Covered in a Cloak of Amnesia," NYT 3/9/09.

circles: on May 23, 2009, at a party conference, Prime Minister Erdoğan admitted for the first time that "[F]or years, those of different identities have been kicked out of our country...this was not done with common sense. This was done with a fascist approach." Although this statement was taken primarily as referring to the Greeks who were expelled, it seems also to have been at least an indirect reference to the fates of other groups, such as the Armenians and the Assyrians.*

A controversial contribution to understanding what happened in 1915 is Guenter Lewy's revisionist review of the historiography, *The Armenian Massacres in Ottoman Turkey: A Disputed Genocide*.† Lewy, who has made something of a reputation as a debunker of genocide claims, including those of Native Americans, states clearly at the beginning of his exploration of the history that he "...endeavored to avoid becoming entangled in problems of definition and nomenclature." This is perhaps a valid position for an historian to take, but it has been disappointing to many Armenian readers and his book has been attacked as inaccurate by other scholars.‡

Professor Lewy asserts that:

> ...the question of what constitutes genocide—whether according to the Genocide Convention approved by the General Assembly of the United Nations on December 9, 1948, or in terms of other rival definitions—is often far from simple; and the attempt to decide whether the Armenian massacres in Ottoman Turkey fit all, some, or none of these definitions strikes me as of limited utility. I have therefore concentrated on what appears to me to be the far more important task of clarifying what happened, how it happened,

---

* Originally reported by Reuter, this comment was the subject of a column on May 28 by Harut Sassounian.

† Guenter Lewy, *The Armenian Massacres in Ottoman Turkey: A Disputed Genocide.* Salt Lake City: University of Utah Press, 2005.

‡ See, e.g., Akçam Taner in *Genocide Studies and Prevention* Volume 3, No. 1, Spring 2008, pp. 111-145.

and why it happened. The issue of the appropriate label to be attached to these occurrences is relevant for the ongoing polemics between Turks and Armenians. It is of secondary importance at best for historical inquiry, because the use of legal nomenclature does not add any material facts important for the history of these events.[*]

Does it really matter, then, whether the awful events of 1915-16 constituted genocide? To some historians it may not – and Lewy conspicuously puts himself in a minority with his hands-off approach – but it should matter to the rest of us. History does matter. Truth does matter. If crimes were committed, that matters. If we care about ethics, if we care about justice, we must attempt to assign values to events, current as well as historical. If we do not, we are shirking our human responsibility and ducking the important issues of our times. While in a perfect world one would prefer that parliaments and legislatures not pass judgments on historical issues, the fact that *denial* of the Armenian Genocide is the official policy of one state (Turkey) poses a special challenge to other states, including the United States. As Donald Bloxham observes:

> The notion of states passing resolutions on the character of historical events is undoubtedly an odd one in any circumstances. Whether something qualifies as an instance of genocide is a matter for scholars of history and the law, not politicians acting as politicians. The fact that genocide is the quintessential state crime only adds piquancy to the issue. There are considerable mitigating factors to official pronouncements adjudicating in the Armenian case, however. The Turkish state has sought to play the game of denial on the international political stage and has therefore invited a response in kind....It is improbable that Ankara will fully address the record of 1915-16 without external pressure.[†]

---

[*] Lewy, op. cit., p. xii.

[†] Bloxham, op. cit., p. 226.

In short, under these conditions, not to counter the official policy of denial means to condone it. Forty-two of our fifty American states have passed resolutions or legislation affirming the Armenian Genocide as such and there is no constitutional or legal bar to the Congress's doing so. The House of Representatives has seen fit to pass resolutions on a multitude of historical issues, including, in 1975 and 1984, on the Armenian Genocide. The Congress is not, as the French, Swiss and Slovak parliaments have done, criminalizing the act of denying the Armenian Genocide.[*] House Resolution 106 was actually quite tame: it did not accuse the Turkish Republic of any crime, nor did it suggest anyone be punished for the Genocide. To raise such heated objections to the resolution, as Turkish representatives did in October, 2007, going so far as to threaten to close the Incirlik air base that supplies American combat forces in Iraq, falls into the category of "protesting too much." House Resolution 106 contained facts and figures that can be quibbled with, and a lengthy critique published in May, 2008 by the Turkish Industrialists' and Businessmens' Association[†] found many minor faults with it, but the broad outlines of the story it told were not inaccurate.

Defining Genocide

The legal definition enshrined in the 1948 Convention quite clearly states the criteria for defining the crime of Genocide, but few of us are clear about those criteria. For those readers who are not familiar with the definition, I reproduce it here:

---

[*] Inasmuch as the French bill on genocide denial has not become law, denying the Armenian Genocide is not illegal in France, and an academic argument (as opposed to "hate speech") would be tolerated also in Switzerland. The European Court's decision in the Perinicek case in October 2015 confirmed this.

[†] *U.S. H. Res. 106: Factual and Legal Deficiencies*. TUSIAD, Istanbul, 2008.

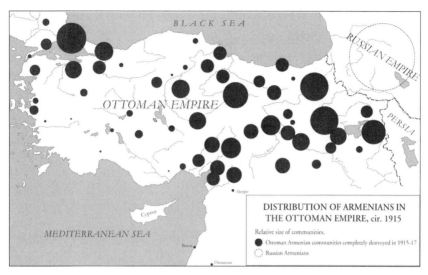

Armenian communities slated for destruction in 1915.

[G]enocide means any of the following acts committed with intent to destroy, in whole or in part, a national, ethnical, racial or religious group, as such:

(a) Killing members of the group;

(b) Causing serious bodily or mental harm to members of the group;

(c) Deliberately inflicting on the group conditions of life calculated to bring about its physical destruction in whole or in part;

(d) Imposing measures intended to prevent births within the group;

(e) Forcibly transferring children of the group to another group.[*]

This is a rather broad definition. Note that it does not require that a specific government or state be identified as the perpetrator – a point that is frequently ignored. It is such a broad definition that it tends to threaten the self-image of many nations that have a bloody history. The United States Senate for forty years delayed ratifying the

* Genocide Convention, Art. II.

Convention in part for fear that its provisions might be turned against, particularly, our Southern states for crimes such as lynching and slavery. Of course, the even older questions of Native American Indians and the history of the European conquest of the Americas, North and South, are also open to interpretation in light of the Convention's provisions. Estimates of the initial native population of North America vary widely, but it is generally accepted that by 1900 it was reduced to approximately 250,000 as a result, direct or indirect, of the European colonization and expansion that started in the fifteenth century.[*] These are uncomfortable facts of our own history.

As was asserted in the aforementioned legal analysis commissioned by the International Center for Transitional Justice, the "[Events of 1915] viewed collectively, can thus be said to include all of the elements of the crime of genocide as defined in the Convention, and legal scholars as well as historians, politicians, journalists and other people would be justified in continuing to so describe them."[†] This is a *non-judicial* use of the term; one might claim, as I did to my superiors at the State Department, to speak of "genocide" in a *historical* sense. The word "genocide" is commonly used by virtually everyone, save utterly cautious governments and international organizations, to describe historical and even current events, without benefit of an officially recognized finding by a court of law.[‡] In unfolding pre-genocidal situations, the criminal justice model, in which the accused is considered innocent until proven guilty, is particularly unsuitable: once the crime has been committed to the satisfaction of a court, it is too late for the victims. Much more

---

[*] See Guenter Lewy, "Were American Indians the Victims of Genocide?" in *Commentary*, 11/22/04.

[†] ICTJ Analysis, p. 4.

[‡] Ottoman courts-martial convened in 1919 did, of course, find the main perpetrators of the Genocide guilty of capital crimes and sentenced the ring-leaders, including Talaat, Enver and Jemal, to death. They had already fled the country, but each was brought to rough justice within the next few years.

appropriate is to apply the "precautionary principle" drawn from medical practice, in which one begins treatment – or prevention – on serious suspicion that the crime may be about to occur. But what about genocides that occurred in the past?

Guenther Lewy has this to say about the "non-judicial" use of the word "genocide":

> As mentioned earlier, some Armenians use the word "genocide" not as a legal concept but as a term of moral opprobrium that castigates the deportation and its attending huge loss of life as a grave moral evil. Paradoxical as it may seem, this way of approaching the problem may offer a way out of the frozen positions. If the Armenians could be persuaded to forego resort to the legal concept of genocide as a systematic and premeditated program of the destruction of a people and be satisfied with a Turkish acknowledgement of sincere regret for the terrible suffering of the Armenian people during the First World War, a path might open toward reconciliation.[*]

Indeed, commentators and political activists have resorted to the use of the term "genocide" more frequently and more loosely than is probably healthy for our debates on the subject.[†] One authority, David Scheffer, has pointed out that the term "genocide" "has been commonly used, particularly in political dialogue, to describe atrocities of great diversity, magnitude and character."[‡] But while the word is in common and ever-more-frequent public usage, governments are wary of it because the 1948 Convention requires that the contracting parties "undertake to prevent and to punish" the crime. Scheffer suggests that "Governments and international

---

[*] Lewy, op. cit., p. 271.

[†] The Merriam-Webster Home and Office Dictionary defines "genocide" as "the deliberate and systematic destruction of a racial, political or cultural group," which is an even broader concept.

[‡] David Scheffer, "Genocide and Atrocity Crimes," in *Genocide Studies and Prevention*, Volume 1, No. 3, December 2006, pp. 229 ff.

organizations should be liberated to apply the term "genocide" more readily within a political context...and should not be constrained from acting by the necessity of a prior legal finding that the crime of genocide in fact has occurred..." In short, the use of the word "genocide" ought not to be a complete taboo, as has been the case in U.S. governmental circles; rather, its usage needs to be sanctioned, at least in a historical and political sense. Scheffer goes on to suggest that, when governments see trouble on the horizon, they ought to feel free to point to "precursors of genocide" without fearing that they will be inexorably drawn into military action to prevent a potential genocide from occurring.*

Scheffer's primary concern, of course, is with current and future genocidal situations: he was the U.S. Ambassador at Large for War Crimes Issues in the Clinton Administration. But what about a ninety-year-plus old case of what looks convincingly like a case of genocide? Shouldn't we call it by that name, even if it has not been recognized as such by an international court? Certainly that is what the legal analysis commissioned by the TARC proposed: "...The Events, viewed collectively, can thus be said to include all of the elements of the crime of genocide as defined in the Convention, and legal scholars as well as historians, politicians, journalists and other people would be justified in continuing to so describe them."†

My answer is an unequivocal "yes."

I believe we – U.S. diplomats as well as ordinary American citizens – must feel free to refer to the Armenian Genocide as such, even if only in a *historical* sense, if not in a strictly *legal* sense. No other term at this point adequately captures the full extent of the horrors that were inflicted on the Armenians. And there is a further consideration: as Charles Isherwood put it in an Op-Ed in the New York *Times*, "...by keeping the words taboo, we unwittingly preserve their power

---

* Ibid., p. 232.

† Turkish Armenian Reconciliation Council, op. cit., Executive Summary, p. 4.

to hurt."[*] By keeping "Armenian Genocide" in the taboo category, we fail to minister to the deep wound to their collective national psyche that Armenians still nourish. By speaking out about it openly, by degrees we may help that wound to heal.

The historian Donald Bloxham has done some of the best thinking about the question of Turkish denial and politicization of the term "genocide." He has identified one crucial reason why the word "genocide" itself is now intrinsic to the debate:

> The political premium that the Turkish state has put on avoiding the "genocide" word has also created a rod for its own back. If it were possible to generate Turkish awareness and acceptance that the Armenians were victims of a state-sponsored programme of mass murder, the use or otherwise of the 'g' word to describe that programme would, all things being equal, be a matter solely for good-faith academic and public debate. Yet so many misrepresentations and falsehoods are tied up with rejection of the applicability of the term that imposing it upon the debate is (unfortunately) probably the only way to create the environment for full Turkish confrontation with the past.[†]

A young woman came up to me at my last appearance at the American University in Armenia in July 2006 and said, "Mr. Ambassador, you have given me back my dignity, and I thank you." I have talked to hundreds of Armenians in both Armenia and the United States. While it is always dangerous to generalize, I believe that simply recognizing the destruction done to their ancestors would help. For the United States and Great Britain to withhold that solace is particularly hurtful, given the remarkable outpouring of sympathy and support that Armenians received from precisely those two countries at the time of the actual events. The United States and Britain are increasingly isolated in maintaining this position. Canada, on the other hand, has courageously moved into the column of those

---

[*] *New York Times*, Dec. 17, 2006.

[†] Bloxham, op. cit., p. 226.

countries recognizing the Armenian genocide. Prime Minister Stephen Harper himself issued a statement that said in part:

> Ninety-one years ago the Armenian people experienced terrible suffering and loss of life. In recent years the Senate of Canada adopted a motion acknowledging this period as "the first genocide of the twentieth century," while the House of Commons adopted a motion that "acknowledges the Armenian genocide of 1915 and condemns this act as a crime against humanity." My party and I supported those resolutions and continue to recognize them today.[*]

Assistant Secretary of State Dan Fried, in testimony before the House Foreign Affairs Committee March 15, 2007, used the term "ethnic cleansing," a first for a State Department official.[†] This statement makes it clear that, even if the events of 1915 did not rise (in the view of successive U.S. administrations) to the level of genocide, they did constitute a crime. Ethnic cleansing is a "crime against humanity," although the term has been described as "genocide from the point of view of the perpetrator," and is not in favor with serious genocide scholars.[‡] Assistant Secretary Fried's statement represented, I believe, a significant step that appears to have gone under-appreciated. This phraseology did not find its way into President Bush's April 24, 2007 or 2008 Presidential Messages, which many Armenian-Americans I have talked to perceived as a step backwards. Marie "Masha" Yovanovitch used the term "ethnic cleansing" during her Senate confirmation hearing, picking up Assistant Secretary Fried's turn of phrase and thus pressing slightly beyond what President Bush had officially said.[**]

---

[*] Statement from Prime Minister on Day of Commemoration of Armenian Genocide, April 19, 2006.

[†] Daniel Fried, testimony on U.S.-Turkish Relations before the HFAC, March 15, 2007.

[‡] Prof. Elihu D. Richter, at the 7th Biennial Conference of the International Association of Genocide Scholars, Sarajevo, Bosnia-Herzogovina, July 12, 2007.

[**] Marie Yovanovitch, testimony before the SFRC, June 19, 2008.

Taner Akçam points out that the question of the Armenian Genocide has become entangled, from the very first days, in the larger question of Turkish statehood. He writes, "The Turkish example shows that there is a sharp – and perhaps irreconcilable – contradiction between the right of states to national sovereignty, on the one hand, and the pursuit and prosecution of crimes against humanity, on the other."* The attempt to bring to justice the main perpetrators of the Genocide ultimately came to naught because the Allies gave precedence to their own national self-interests. Ultimately, it seems to me, the issues of Turkish sovereignty and territorial integrity – the achievements of Atatürk's resistance and revolution – need to be disentangled from the question of the Genocide, and treated separately. Only when Turks feel secure in their statehood, within boundaries that are not challenged, will they feel confident enough to begin dealing with the Armenian Genocide on the requisite scale. Those who argue that "...if the Armenian, as well as the Greek and Assyrian Genocides are recognized, Turkey will stop existing as a State"† are not helping to bring recognition about; they are impeding it. In fact, any lasting solution to the long-standing dispute between Turks and Armenians has to be ultimately comforting to both sides. And that obviously remains a very tall order.

Another issue that needs to be separated from the historical question of the Armenian Genocide is that of U.S. national interests. As Senator Biden once told Reuters, "A relationship that rests on a requirement of a denial of an historical event, [that] is not a sound basis for a relationship."‡ Surely the United States has important interests in the Near East and in the bilateral relationship with Ankara, but, as Robert Fisk has put it, "The problem is, if the Western governments, including the United States, stood up to the Turks and said they must acknowledge it [the Armenian Genocide], they would. But since they don't, the Turks don't have to. They get

---

* Akçam, op. cit., p. 371.

† PanArmenian.Net analytical department posting dated March 21, 2007.

‡ Reuters wire report dated March 28, 2007, datelined Washington.

Khor Virap monastery with the biblical Mount Ararat in the background.

away with it."[*] If we are to be true friends of the Turks, we ought not to be hindering their slow and halting but, one hopes, inevitable progress toward facing and acknowledging the uncomfortable facts of their past. The State Department has argued that "…the tragic events of 1915 are of such human significance that their characterization should be determined not by political decisions." Precisely my point: governments, including our own, ought not to be making a political decision that the events of 1915 were *not* "genocide" especially when the majority of historians and specialists, outside of Turkey, are convinced they were. The decision *not* to call the Genocide "genocide" is itself a political decision.

Just hours before the July 29, 2008 SFRC vote on Marie Yovanovitch's nomination to be the next U.S. Ambassador to Yerevan, the State Department wrote to Senator Biden to say that "…the Administration recognizes that the mass killings, ethnic cleansing, and forced deportation of over one and a half million

* Robert Fisk, Middle East correspondent of *The Independent*, interviewed by *The Armenian Reporter* and quoted March 19, 2007 by PanArmenian.net.

Armenians were conducted by the Ottoman Empire. We indeed hold Ottoman officials responsible for those crimes."

This was major progress, if not a victory. Full U.S. recognition of the events of 1915-16 will eventually happen, as even the arch-realist Henry Kissinger reportedly once said,[*] but more than simple recognition is needed, and we Americans ought to think about it now. In the final part of this book, I will suggest a few things that could and should be done.

---

[*] Carissa Vanitzian, "Two Questions to Henry Kissinger," ANN/Groong, April 22, 1998.

Part III

. . . And Us

What is to be Done?

Lenin's (and Cherneshevskiy's) second question – the first being, "who is guilty?" – is seemingly always in order. But, in this case, there is a prior question that needs to be explored.

If Genocide recognition comes, what will it mean? Some Armenians fear that it *will come* and have *zero consequences*. Some Armenians of my acquaintance do not even want to discuss the question for this reason. A few actually found my statements in 2005 troubling because of it. They worry that the worldwide identity of the ten or so million far-flung Armenians depends on the struggle for Genocide recognition, and may vanish if recognition is achieved. Some scholars and activists fear that Genocide recognition without meaningful consequences will simply signal, once again, that states and other groups can feel free to perpetrate genocide without fear of serious consequences.

It needs to be said – and probably a non-Armenian needs to say it – that Armenians themselves are reluctant to discuss the question of what they really want, beyond the minimum demand of "recognition," on which all agree. Dennis Papazian, a senior Armenian scholar in Dearborn, Michigan, put it this way: "…any Armenian commentator who tries to second-guess the Armenian public is stepping out on a slippery slope. No matter what they might advise, there is no question that they will be subject to heated and bitter criticism from one quarter or another. I certainly would never consider going down that road. It would be public suicide."[*] I am conscious that not all of my Armenian friends will appreciate what I have to say below; certainly my Turkish friends will not be entirely happy either. But the subject needs to be discussed and debated.

[*] Dennis R. Papazian, "Thoughts on Armenian-Turkish Relations," in *The Armenian Weekly*, April 26, 2008, p. 44.

It seems to me clear that, for a number of reasons, the Armenian Genocide of 1915-16 is very difficult now to prosecute or punish as a crime. What court would hear the case? Some suggest the World Court – the International Court of Justice or ICJ – at The Hague. But not only is the Republic of Turkey highly unlikely to submit to the jurisdiction of the ICJ – and under the normal rules of the Court, both parties must do so – but there are serious doubts as to how any claim could successfully be pressed under the 1948 Convention. The legal principle, "*nullum crimen sine lege, nulla poena sine lege praevia*"* comes into play here. Alfred de Zayas has, of course, argued that the 1948 Convention simply codified previously existing international law. In the most recent version of his argument, he points out that under Article IX of the Genocide Convention, any State party can submit a "contentious case" to the International Court of Justice and request a determination "relating to the responsibility of a State for genocide." If the Court's jurisdiction were challenged, it could be argued in response that the Turkish Government's continuing denial of the genocide constituted a persistent attack on the human dignity of the Armenian people and that the damages done to them have continued down to the present day.†

There is an additional impediment to a court-based solution of the problem. The United States took almost forty years to ratify the Genocide Convention, finally doing so under the persistent pressure of the late Senator William Proxmire, who rose more than 3,000 times in the Senate Chamber to urge its ratification. It was a confluence of events in 1986 that brought about U.S. ratification, and when it finally happened, the Chairman of the Senate Foreign Relations Committee, Richard Lugar (R – Indiana) proposed "reservations" to the ratification. These "reservations" are defined as

---

* Lat., literally, "no crime without law, no punishment without previous law."

† Alfred de Zayas, "The Armenian Genocide in the Light of the Genocide Convention," Nicosia: April 2008 and forthcoming in *The Armenian Review*.

"unilateral declarations that excluded or modified terms of the treaty and affected only the party entering the reservation." The United States claimed in this way the "right to refuse jurisdiction when it determined that going before the World Court would not be in the national interest." This of course protects the U.S. from harassment cases, but it also provides an easy excuse for another nation to resist U.S. jurisdiction, and could be used by another state to stay clear of the Court. In the U.S. version of the Convention, whose provisions were taken into U.S. law, persons who commit the crime of genocide should be punished, whether "constitutionally responsible rulers, public officials or private individuals." What is of interest here is that the crime does not have to be committed by the State; it is sufficient for individuals to have genocidal intent and to act on it in certain defined ways. [*]

But this brings up another point. All of the real-life perpetrators of the massacres and deportations of the period 1915-16 are certainly now dead. Even the youngest of the Nazi-era war criminals, a generation younger than the Young Turks, are nearly all gone by this time. So whom might one prosecute? It is true that the Republic of Turkey is the successor state to the Ottoman Empire, and, according to another legal principle, *"res transit cum onere suo."*[†] But sons are not guilty for the crimes of their fathers (or in this case, grandfathers). The crime of genocide was meant to be punished by prosecuting specific individuals. In fact, the 1948 Genocide Convention provides that "persons," rather than states, shall be *punished* for the crime of genocide, although it does also provide for consideration of the "responsibility of a State for genocide."[‡]

I have discussed with many Armenian friends the hard facts that militate against the more ambitious goals – return of lands in

---

* Congressional Quarterly Almanac, 1986, pp. 383-3.

† Lat., literally, "the thing transits with its own burden," that is, the rights and obligations of the previous state convey to the successor state.

‡ U.N. Convention on the Prevention and Punishment of the Crime of Genocide, Articles IV and IX.

BOUNDARY BETWEEN TURKEY AND ARMENIA
AS DETERMINED BY
WOODROW WILSON, PRESIDENT OF THE UNITED STATES OF AMERICA

President Woodrow Wilson's Arbitral Award.

"Western Armenia," by which is meant eastern Turkey – that some of them still harbor. First of all, there is the 1923 Treaty of Lausanne, which established the modern Republic of Turkey within its present-day borders. The earlier (1920) Treaty of Sèvres that provided for an Armenian state in Asia Minor within borders determined by Woodrow Wilson was never ratified and is now clearly defunct.

But there are many more recent barriers to the dreams of acquiring territory from Turkey. One is the 1949 Treaty of Washington that established the North Atlantic Alliance, which Turkey (and Greece) joined in 1952. Article IV of that treaty refers to the "territorial integrity" of the States signatory, and the following article, the famous Article V, commits each of the signatory powers to treat an attack on the territory of any of the Alliance's members as an attack upon itself. A more recent international instrument was the 1975 Helsinki Final Act, which also recognized the territorial integrity of the CSCE Participating States. There are, in fact, so many international agreements that bolster the territorial integrity of the Republic of Turkey that it might be the better part of valor for Armenians, wherever located, to quietly drop their quest to obtain territory at Turkey's expense. As Taner Akçam said to an audience at Harvard, "The question of territory should be considered closed and resolved…"[*]

Harut Sassounian has, in the pages of the California *Courier* that he publishes, eloquently called for Armenians never to forget that their lands were usurped, and not to give up their claim for the traditional "three R's:" "recognition, reparations and restitution." But Harut goes farther and argues that, since recognition of the Genocide has already effectively been accomplished – even though neither Turkey nor the United States nor Great Britain recognizes the 1915 Events as genocide – it is time to move on to the second goal, reparations. As for the question of territory, he advocates "keeping the hope and dream alive for succeeding generations of Armenians that someday they will regain their historic lands…the way the Jews did by proclaiming 'next year in Jerusalem' for two thousand years."[†] While this is perhaps inspiring to some Armenians, it is no doubt equally frightening to most Turks, and seems to me a formula for virtually endless conflict. Do we really want that? Might it not be better for Armenians to heed the famous words of the French politician Léon Gambetta concerning Alsace-Lorraine after France's defeat in the Franco-Prussian War, "Pensez-y toujours, parlez-en jamais"?[‡] But this is a difficult question that Armenians will have to

---

[*] Harvard Crimson on-line, 3/15/2007. Akçam went on to say that "…the question of responsibility [for the Genocide] and human rights abuses should be considered unresolved."

[†] California *Courier*, December 6, 2007.

[‡] "Think of it always, speak of it never."

resolve for themselves. The gradual democratic evolution of Turkey may change the nature of the question over time.

A somewhat less extreme version of the "Sèvres Settlement" dream is the hope nourished by some Armenians to get "at least Mt. Ararat" back from Turkey. Though a seemingly more moderate goal, this is, frankly, very unlikely. No state in modern times has willingly given up territory without some form of armed conflict. The one contrary example I am aware of is Czechoslovakia and its 1993 "velvet divorce" into Czech and Slovak Republics, which my wife and I witnessed while serving in Prague at that time.* The other example that might be cited is the U.S. agreement to give up control of the Panama Canal.†

The most reasonable goal, it seems to me, is to engineer better political relations between Armenia and Turkey – including Armenians and Turks abroad – and gradually allow the importance of the Turkish-Armenian border to fade away into insignificance. If the closed border were opened to tourism and trade, it could, in time, become a source of stability and greater prosperity for the populations of both eastern Turkey and the Republic of Armenia. Yerevan could easily emerge as an economic magnet for eastern Anatolia. Armenians understandably love and revere Mt. Ararat, whose "sister" mountain, Aragats, is in Armenia; but only by waging peace and diplomacy, not through pressure and propaganda, is Ararat likely to become an easily accessible destination for tourists and other pilgrims. At some future point, if relations between Turkey and Armenia reach a degree of mutual trust, it might be possible to imagine cooperation and even a special regime to encourage restoration of Armenian cultural monuments and subsequently Armenian tourism in the ancient Armenian capital city of Ani.

---

* It was an unusual experience to have a country change its borders right under one's feet, but that is what happened on New Year's Day, 2003. We thought both Czechs and Slovaks profited from their "divorce."

† Alex van Oss points out that Finland declined to recover Karelia and Petsamo after WWII.

Clearly it will not be enough for many Armenians, descendants of survivors of the Genocide, for the awful events of 1915-16 – some extend the period to 1923 – simply to be recognized as "genocide," although that would certainly be a positive step, and a great moral victory. This has, in fact, been the goal of the Government of the Republic of Armenia: as stated by former Foreign Minister Oskanian, "Armenia's foreign policy agenda includes the recognition of Genocide only."[*] But note that when President Sargsyan speaks, as he did in December, 2011, about "justice," one has to assume that Armenians of various political persuasions will read into that word what they wish. In July 2013, addressing a conference of lawyers in Yerevan, Armenia's Prosecutor General suggested that a legal case for recovering "lost lands" ought to be prepared against Turkey. Sadly, it seems to me that international law is not going to provide a solution, however clever and well-grounded the legal case might be. The issue is in a domain that requires political and diplomatic, rather than legal, approaches.

It is not unreasonable for the Republic of Armenia to seek recognition of the Genocide for the sake of its own security. Diplomatic relations with Turkey and reopening of the closed border are important short term goals, but Turkey's continuing denial of the Genocide poses a subtle long-term threat to Armenia's existence. Consider what Donald Bloxham has said on this subject: "Since denial has always been accompanied by rhetoric of Armenian treachery, aggression, criminality, and territorial ambition, it actually enunciates an ongoing if latent threat of Turkish 'revenge.' It would be difficult to imagine the Armenian state feeling safe in its relations with a Turkish state that continued to subscribe to some of the canards used to rationalize the destruction of 1915-16."[†]

Survivors of the Armenian Genocide are now, sadly, very few. They and their survivors now living dispersed in countries around the

---

[*] As stated to Agence France Press, according to RFE/RL on Nov. 27, 2006.

[†] Bloxham, op. cit., p. 234.

world claim, with moral justification, that there ought to be "reparations," or at least some compensation or redress for what was done to their ancestors and relatives. This is easy to say, and to agree with, but very difficult to accomplish under present circumstances. In an effort to grapple with this challenge, the University of Southern California's Institute of Armenian Studies convened a number of legal scholars to discuss International Law and the Armenian Genocide in September 2007. While there was no clear consensus, several speakers pointed out how difficult it had been even for survivors of the Nazi Holocaust to obtain compensation, although the lapse of time in their case was much shorter and the documentation much better than in the case of the 1915 Genocide. Some limited success in obtaining a measure of redress for Armenians has been achieved in class action suits against insurance companies (e.g., New York Life and the French firm AXA) and there is a case pending against Deutsche Bank, but these are secondary targets and only partial victories. Taking the Turkish State to court for the 1915 Genocide would be a prodigious and, as we have discussed already, probably unsuccessful undertaking in current circumstances. Still, some effort at providing a modicum of justice for the Armenians appears justified. So, what can realistically be done? How can we Americans help?

Ten Modest Proposals

Establishing among the broad public the truth of what happened in 1915-16 has to come first. So long as there are lingering doubts about the basic history, the pursuit of anything approaching "justice" will remain difficult. This is undoubtedly the calculation of those who participate in the denial and suppression of the facts of the matter. It is probably sufficient from their point of view simply to obfuscate and raise questions, so as to block any effort to make amends. Even if, as I believe to be the case, the facts of the matter have by now been more than adequately established in the "court of public opinion," not to mention the "jury of historians and genocide scholars," the

United States Capitol, the seat of the United States Congress.

unforgiving geopolitical facts of today's world will continue to play an important, possibly even decisive role, in such matters. But still, it seems to me, there are some practical approaches that can be considered. None of these approaches will magically solve the complex problem posed by the reality of the Armenian Genocide, but together they might encourage the Turkish state to come to grips more honestly with the facts of history and in the meantime give some psychological and material relief to Armenians.

1. The U.S. Congress should not fear to pass the Resolutions on the Armenian Genocide, H. Res. 106 and S. Res. 106, or successor resolutions (H. Res. 304 and S. Res. 399) that may be introduced in the Congress. In early October, 2007, some 226 members of the House of Representatives were on record as favoring this non-binding, but significant, statement,* and, on October 10, it was approved by the House Foreign Affairs Committee by a vote of 27 to 21. Committee Chairman Tom Lantos, until his death in 2008 the

* The text of the current resolution can be found at www.house.gov.

sole Holocaust survivor in the U.S. Congress, cast his vote for it. But then, in a virtual tsunami of rejection, no fewer than eight former Secretaries of State and three former Secretaries of Defense, as well as the Government of Turkey, the President of the United States and the majority of American foreign policy commentators came out in strong opposition to the resolution, the official title of which was "Affirmation of the United States Record on the Armenian Genocide." Its consideration was put on hold indefinitely. This should really have surprised no one, including Speaker Nancy Pelosi, who has long favored the bill, but it did. Resistance to employing the word "genocide" with regard to the events of 1915 on the part of the Government of Turkey and the U.S. Government is deeply ingrained and the pattern of denial actually goes back to before the word "genocide" even existed.[*] The timing of consideration of the resolution – always bad, given repeated Turkish threats of retaliation – could hardly have been worse, with the Turkish General Staff and other Turkish officials this time in a position credibly to threaten military action across the Iraqi border (against the Kurds) and withdrawal of crucial support for U.S. forces engaged in Iraq.

What was notable was that almost no commentator or Member of Congress actually questioned the fact that there had been a genocide of the Armenians in 1915-16. In a column in the Washington *Post*, the conservative columnist Charles Krauthammer, while admitting "unequivocally" that the Armenian Genocide was a "matter of simple historical record," went on to say that to pass a "declarative resolution in the House of Representatives in the middle of a war in which we are inordinately dependent on Turkey would be the height of irresponsibility."[†] Granted, if one's sole point of reference is hard,

---

[*] According to Donald Bloxham, op. cit., p. 207, "Genocide denial was entrenched before the word genocide was coined because initially denial of what had happened to the Armenians was directly related to the historical Armenian question at a political level."

[†] Charles Krauthammer, "Pelosi's Armenian Gambit," The Washington *Post*, October 19, 2007.

cold, U.S. interests and one's guiding philosophy is *Realpolitik*, it is indeed difficult to imagine a moment when such a resolution would seem to be advisable; however, U.S. policy ought not to be based exclusively on hard, cold interests and *Realpolitik*. But even leaving aside the ethical considerations, if one must, international politics does occasionally provide openings. The tactical moment for pushing through a difficult decision can sometimes arise when the relevant party makes a policy decision that calls for an appropriate reaction. Such a moment arose when the Greek Cypriot community, in early 2004, rejected the Kofi Annan plan for Cyprus. Shortly after that, Washington first used the term "Macedonia" for the state that previously, out of deference to Athens, had been awkwardly labeled the "Former Yugoslav Republic of Macedonia." The Turkish National Assembly's refusal to grant passage to U.S. armed forces seeking to enter northern Iraq in March 2003 brought about the change of Rep. Lantos's vote to the "yes" column on the Armenian Genocide resolution that was then in play. Were the Turkish Generals – or the so-called "deep state" – to step in and commit an anti-democratic *coup d'état* against the mildly Islamist Justice and Development Party (AKP), arguably the best government Turkey had had for years, that could produce the right political moment to pass the resolution, although it would come at a terrible cost to Turkey's democracy. The HFAC again passed the resolution in March 2010, by one vote, but in the waning days of the 211th Congress, Speaker Pelosi and Deputy Speaker Hoyer decided not to put it to a floor vote. Simply maintaining reasonable pressure on Turkey to come to terms with the facts, while allowing domestic progressive forces to gradually open up the possibilities for coming to terms with history, seems to me the best course of action.

2. Museum of Armenian History and Culture, and Genocide Memorial, located in Washington. In 2000 several prominent Armenian-Americans acquired the handsome former building of the Bank of Washington at 14th and G Streets to house such a museum, although complicated legal disputes and the prolonged economic

downturn undermined the effort. Nevertheless, such a museum, in my view, could still materialize not only as a place for the display of cultural artifacts (of which the Armenians have many, and of high quality) but a platform for the arts, music, drama and dance, as well as a center for study of the history and culture of Armenia, including the Genocide. On the model of the Smithsonian's National Museum of the American Indian, it could provide a setting in which the Armenian-American community might hold commemorative events and social gatherings. It could contain a bookshop and a café or restaurant featuring Armenian coffee and cuisine. Benefactors' names could be prominently displayed, and, "righteous," or at least penitent, Turks, maybe even – someday – the Government of the Republic of Turkey, listed among them. Contributions to such an institution would constitute an act of piety, sympathy or contrition, depending on the donor's relationship to the historical record. As in the case of the National Museum of the American Indian, such a museum would allow Armenian-Americans to tell their story as they want to tell it, a telling that has been largely denied to them. Virginia Congressman Jim Moran has also proposed establishment of a Museum of the American People, and Armenians should surely be represented there.

3. The President of the United States, in the tradition of both Woodrow Wilson and Ronald Reagan, should recognize the Armenian Genocide as an historical fact. The United States has in fact already done so in the 1951 filing before the World Court quoted at the beginning of Part II. The United States is both a moral beacon to the world and a power with concrete and specific, down-to-earth interests. In principle, we should stand on the side of acknowledging the truth, and certainly should not collude in its denial. As an interim step, the President's next annual Proclamation should *at a minimum* recognize that the vast preponderance of historians and experts consider the 1915 massacres of Armenians to be a case of "genocide." This could be accomplished simply by putting that fact into a subordinate clause or into parentheses. It

might go something like this: "…the history of Ottoman attacks against Armenians (which most scholars believe constitute genocide)…" These words in quotation marks are not my invention: they are lifted verbatim from the website of the Holocaust Museum in Washington.* Such a formulation would at least recognize the vast majority opinion of American and other scholars, and of international "civil society," without requiring the U.S. Government to adopt a formal, legal position of its own on the matter, if, for foreign policy reasons involving Turkey, it somehow cannot bring itself to do so. I proposed a variation of this solution to Deputy Assistant Secretary of State for European Affairs Matthew Bryza on March 8, 2006. My suggestion was to have the President say "…we regret the Armenian tragedy, *which many scholars consider to have been a case of genocide,* and we call on both sides…etc." As I explained to Matt, this wording "would recognize that there is a respectable body of scholarly opinion that has come to a conclusion, and in this way would take a step in the direction of more intellectual honesty, while preserving the U.S.G.'s hallowed tradition of not having formally made up its mind." This indirect formulation went too far for the State Department in 2006, but it might yet come in handy as a half-step forward on the way to full recognition.

President Obama was widely expected to use the word "genocide" in his annual proclamation on April 24, 2009, but he did not, which was poorly received by many if not most Armenian-Americans. Candidate Obama was on record, not only in his July 2006 letter to Secretary Rice, but in campaign statements and literature, as believing that the 1915-16 massacres of Armenians constituted genocide. Furthermore, Candidate Obama had said "America deserves a leader who speaks truthfully about the Armenian genocide and responds forcefully to all genocides. I intend to be that leader."

---

* Holocaust Museum and Memorial. *www.ushmm.org*. From "home" go to "Holocaust Encyclopedia" then "What is Genocide?" and "Genocide Timeline."

In early April, 2009, President Obama visited Turkey. In his address to the Turkish parliament on April 6, the President spoke of the challenge facing "all democracies" of how they deal with the past, and he cited America's "legacies of slavery and segregation, the past treatment of Native Americans." He went on to say:

> Human endeavor is by its nature imperfect. History is often tragic, but unresolved, it can be a heavy weight. Each country must work through its past. And reckoning with the past can help us seize a better future. I know there's strong views in this chamber about the terrible events of 1915. And while there's been a good deal of commentary about my views, it's really about how the Turkish and Armenian people deal with the past. And the best way forward for the Turkish and Armenian people is a process that works through the past in a way that is honest, open and constructive.

Later in his Turkish visit the President participated in a press availability and responded to the following question from Christi Parsons of the Chicago *Tribune*:

> Parsons: Mr. President, as a U.S. senator you stood with the Armenian-American community in calling for Turkey's acknowledgement of the Armenian Genocide and you also supported the passage of the Armenian Genocide resolution. You said as president you would recognize the Genocide. And my question for you is, have you changed your views and did you ask President Gül to recognize the Genocide by name?

The President answered as follows:

> Well, my views are on the record and I have not changed views. What I have been very encouraged by is news that under President Gül's leadership, you are seeing a series of negotiations, a process, in place between Armenia and Turkey to resolve a whole host of longstanding issues, including this one.
>
> I want to be as encouraging as possible around those negotiations which are moving forward and could bear fruit

very quickly, very soon. And so as a consequence, what I want to do is not focus on my view right now but focus on the views of the Turkish and the Armenian people. If they can move forward and deal with a difficult and tragic history, then I think the entire world should encourage them…

While the President did not use the word "genocide" in Turkey, no one listening missed the point. President Obama's views had been widely reported in Turkey during the election campaign, and the fact that Obama said he had not changed his views was not lost on the Turks, who watched the proceedings on national television. While American mainstream media reported that President Obama had "side-stepped" the issue, the reality is that he confronted it in a way that was clear and unmistakable to his Turkish audiences and yet courteous and not unnecessarily offensive to them as his hosts. More suspect, in the eyes of Armenian-Americans, was the President's having apparently accepted at face value the Turkish President's assertion that progress was being made in Turkish-Armenian relations. There has so far been little evidence subsequent to the visit that significant progress has been registered.

The President's April 24 statement deserves to be reproduced in full, as it represents incremental progress, even though it does not employ the term "genocide."

> Ninety four years ago, one of the great atrocities of the 20th century began. Each year, we pause to remember the 1.5 million Armenians who were subsequently massacred or marched to their death in the final days of the Ottoman Empire. The *Meds Yeghern* must live on in our memories, just as it lives on in the hearts of the Armenian people.
>
> History, unresolved, can be a heavy weight. Just as the terrible events of 1915 remind us of the dark prospect of man's inhumanity to man, reckoning with the past holds out the powerful promise of reconciliation. I have consistently stated my own view of what occurred in 1915, and my view of that

history has not changed. My interest remains the achievement of a full, frank and just acknowledgement of the facts.

The best way to advance that goal right now is for the Armenian and Turkish people to address the facts of the past as a part of their efforts to move forward. I strongly support efforts by the Turkish and Armenian people to work through this painful history in a way that is honest, open and constructive. To that end, there has been courageous and important dialogue among Armenians and Turks, and within Turkey itself. I also strongly support the efforts by Turkey and Armenia to normalize their bilateral relations. Under Swiss auspices, the two governments have agreed on a framework and roadmap for normalization. I commend this progress and urge them to fulfill its promise.

Together, Armenia and Turkey can forge a relationship that is peaceful, productive and prosperous. And together, the Armenian and Turkish people will be stronger as they acknowledge their common history and recognize their common humanity.

Nothing can bring back those who were lost in the *Meds Yeghern*. But the contributions that Armenians have made over the last ninety-four years stand as a testament to the talent, dynamism and resilience of the Armenian people, and as the ultimate rebuke to those who tried to destroy them. The United States of America is a far richer country because of the many Americans of Armenians descent who have contributed to our society, many of whom immigrated to this country in the aftermath of 1915. Today, I stand with them and with Armenians everywhere with a sense of friendship, solidarity and deep respect.

Armenian critics of the President's statement noted that "Meds Yeghern" is not the Armenian word for genocide (which is *tseghasbanutiun*) and means nothing to non-Armenian speakers, even to many diasporan Armenians. It is a term meaning "Great Catastrophe" that was used in earlier years by an older generation. Its use by the President was seen as yet another, more elegant, cross-cultural euphemism. As Harut Sassounian bitterly put it in his column "Et Tu Obama? Letter from a Former Admirer," "[N]ot only did your aides come up with the wrong Armenian word, but they failed to provide its English translation, so that non-Armenians could understand its meaning. What was, after all, the point of using an Armenian word in an English text? Did your staff run out of English euphemisms for genocide?"[*]

4. The U.S. ambassador should be authorized to speak openly and sincerely at the annual commemoration of the tragedy at the Genocide Memorial in Yerevan. The continued silence of the United States on the subject is hurtful to Armenians worldwide. As Donald Bloxham has written, "The massive trauma inflicted on the collective consciousness of the Armenian people is an open wound, continually aggravated by the refusal to acknowledge its infliction."[†] No U.S. Ambassador to Israel could reasonably be expected to carry out his responsibilities while denying – or even remaining silent about – the Holocaust. It is simply unreasonable to expect a U.S. Ambassador to Yerevan to deny the Armenian Genocide. As a next step, a high political representative of the United States should visit the Genocide Memorial in Yerevan in person, and pronounce appropriate words of respect. Up to now, although the Republic of Armenia is more than twenty years old, no U.S. President or Vice President has yet visited Yerevan.[‡] It was encouraging that the new Assistant Secretary of State for European Affairs, Dr. Philip Gordon, privately visited the Genocide Memorial in Yerevan in June, 2009,[**] but a private visit is

---

[*] The California *Courier*, April 30, 2009.

[†] Bloxham, op. cit., p. 234.

[‡] That no top U.S. official has yet visited Armenia has much to do with the fact that talks on resolving the Nagorno-Karabakh conflict are still going on, so far without success. Were a settlement of that conflict to be achieved, it would clear the way for a high-level visit to both Yerevan and Baku.

[**] Gordon was reported by Armenian media to have made this "private" visit during his stop in Yerevan on June 9, 2009, and to have referred to the Tsitsernakaberd complex as the "Genocide Museum."

insufficient: it is "off the record." More notably still, Secretary of State Hillary Clinton visited the Genocide Memorial in Yerevan during her July 4, 2010 visit. Although the visit was technically closed to the press, a video of her walking with Museum director Haik Demoyan soon surfaced, and it was noted that the wreath Secretary Clinton laid bore a ribbon identifying it as "from the Secretary of State."

5. There is nothing that would do more to improve the overall atmosphere between Armenians and Turks than for Ankara and Yerevan simply to establish normal diplomatic relations without any preconditions. In my time in Yerevan, it became clear that the "megaphone diplomacy" that both sides resorted to was not conveying clear, precise messages in either direction. There was persistent misunderstanding on the part of the Turks about Armenia's alleged "claim" to a portion of Eastern Turkey – the territory that was set aside for Armenia by President Wilson in his arbitral award – and there seemed to me to be an exaggerated fear among Armenians of the true intentions and ambitions of the modern-day Republic of Turkey. The two countries have had sporadic diplomatic contacts at both the Foreign Minister and Deputy Foreign Minister levels, including secret discussions in Switzerland in 2008, but those talks proved largely sterile. In addition, the two countries have official contacts through the Black Sea Economic Forum, headquartered in Istanbul, and via their respective embassies in Tbilisi, in neighboring Georgia. Still, there is no substitute for direct diplomatic contacts, through fully-staffed embassies. As Serzh Sargsyan, then Defense Minister, more recently Prime Minister and now President, put it, "The statehood that both Armenia and Turkey enjoy is not an apartment. You cannot sell it and leave it. Neither Turks nor Armenians will leave the region. The logical solution is to have normal relations with each other. That's what neighbors seek to do in today's world."[*] President Sargsyan startled everyone in 2008 when he invited Turkish President Abdullah Gül to watch a football qualifying match in Yerevan in September 2009. This

---

[*] The *Wall Street Journal*, December 22, 2006.

Secretary of State Clinton and Ambassador Yovanovich at Tsitsernakaberd.

launched a Swiss-mediated effort to induce Ankara and Yerevan to sign and then ratify a set of "Protocols" that would have established diplomatic relations and opened the border according to a strict schedule.

Unfortunately, what the two sides attempted to do ran afoul of opposition on the part of Azerbaijan, a part of whose internationally recognized territory is disputed by the Armenians of Nagorno-Karabakh. I also think that the two sides attempted to do too much and made mistakes in the way they handled it. As of the end of 2011, the process represented by the Protocols seemed to be effectively in a dead end. A much more effective approach would be for the two sides simply to authorize an exchange of diplomatic notes declaring, with no particular fanfare, that they were as of that date in a state of diplomatic relations. This could even be done at the ambassadorial level, and would not affect the legal claims that both sides profess.

Turkey has more than once stated that it has two "preconditions" for establishing diplomatic relations with Armenia: first, that the Nagorno-Karabakh conflict be resolved; and, second, that Armenia cease seeking international recognition of the Armenian Genocide. Serious efforts are currently underway under the auspices of the Minsk Group of the Organization for Security and Cooperation in Europe, of which Turkey is a member, to resolve the Karabakh problem through mediated negotiations. As for dropping its quest for international recognition of the Genocide, this is not a realistic possibility for any elected government of the Republic of Armenia. As the newly-elected President of Armenia, Serzh Sargsyan, and former Parliamentary Speaker Artur Baghdasaryan jointly wrote in the Washington *Post*, "We will also continue to ask the international community to recognize the Armenian genocide, though this issue should not prevent us from moving forward."[*] This is a reasonable position and Turkey ought to find a way to meet the Armenians halfway, even at the risk of being accused of "betrayal" by Azerbaijan.

---

* The Washington *Post*, March 17, 2008, p. A17.

Diplomatic relations do not require agreement on every issue, but they do facilitate accurate communication. For Turkey simply to drop its current precondition that Armenia cease to seek international recognition of the Genocide would be a powerful message in itself.

One day, diplomatic relations are sure to be established, and the sooner, the better. Both sides would do well, even before then, to be alert for opportunities to practice the sort of "earthquake diplomacy" that the Government of Greece undertook in August 1999 when a terrible quake struck parts of Turkey. The Greeks immediately and without hesitation offered to send assistance. A month later, an earthquake struck Athens, and the Turks had a chance to reciprocate, with lasting effects for Greek-Turkish relations.[*] In time, Ankara, working with Yerevan, might visit the idea of setting up a "peace park," along the lines of the Waterton Lakes-Glacier International Peace Park that spans the U.S.-Canada border, encompassing Mt. Ararat and the historic Armenian capital city of Ani, both of which are very close to the shared border. The potential for developing cross-border tourism and nurturing local cross-border trade is significant.

6. Turkey should acknowledge what was done to the Armenians. Today's Republic of Turkey may not be directly responsible for the Genocide, but as the successor state to the defunct Ottoman Empire, it represents a continuing enterprise of Turkish statecraft dating back almost a millennium. Although the founder of the Turkish Republic, Kemal Atatürk, was not himself a direct perpetrator of the Armenian Genocide, many of those who flocked to his nationalist banner in the early 1920s had themselves been involved, and the Turkish State's continuing denial of the scope and nature of the massacres arguably

---

[*] I tried to stimulate a bit of "bird flu diplomacy" on the part of Yerevan during the outbreak of avian influenza that affected several villages in eastern Turkey in late December 2005. Unfortunately, the Armenians chose not to seize the opportunity, but there probably will be outbreaks of this disease in the future, with corresponding chances to take advantage of them. Neither Armenia nor Turkey is immune to bird flu – the closed border is hardly an obstacle to migrating waterfowl – and the two sides have every reason to collaborate in world-wide efforts to prevent a human flu pandemic.

makes it to some degree complicit in the acts undertaken by an earlier generation. Rather than spending millions on lobbyists' fees every year in an increasingly futile effort to block Congressional resolutions recognizing the Armenian Genocide, Turkey would be better served by coming clean on the historical record, fully opening its archives, and taking steps to atone for the crime, without waiting for every parliament in the world to pass such a resolution. The court of international public opinion has already found the Turks' Ottoman ancestors guilty of genocide. Better to recognize this reality and deal with it in a responsible way, as Germany, to its lasting credit, has done in the case of the Holocaust, than to cling to the strategy of denial, which is becoming less credible with each passing year. Turkey's inordinate fears of being held responsible for reparations, or, down the road, territorial concessions, is undoubtedly a major factor in its continuing policy of denial. These fears are exaggerated. But Turkey would gain immeasurably in international stature by admitting the crimes of the past and dedicating a significant sum of money to a public fund for at least partially compensating descendants of Genocide survivors, or Armenian charitable and religious organizations. As the state with the sixteenth largest Gross Domestic Product in the world, Turkey can afford to do this. Recent positive domestic political developments give hope that the ideological strait-jacket of Kemalist orthodoxy may eventually be supplanted by a more flexible, tolerant and realistic approach by Turkey's elected leaders.[*] In pondering this suggestion, though, Turkish leaders should keep in mind that a curt, or inadequate, apology only worsens the original affront. Any acknowledgement – or apology – ought to be full and not susceptible to interpretation as "mere words." Words backed up by deeds, or by financial resources, mean a lot more.

---

[*] As of this writing, the Supreme Court of Turkey had agreed to hear a case in which the leaders of the AKP were being accused of betraying Atatürk's legacy by permitting headscarves at universities.

7. Even before the Genocide has been acknowledged by the Republic of Turkey, which, let's face it, may take a long time, the United States could make a low-key offer to help Turkey restore the few remaining Armenian cultural monuments in Asia Minor, by using the existing mechanism of the U.S. Commission for the Preservation of America's Heritage Abroad. There is nothing in the legislative charter of this little-known Commission to prevent its being used for this purpose; however, the consent, indeed the active cooperation, of the host country is necessary. At my suggestion, the Commission, under the leadership of its Chairman, Warren L. Miller, participated in funding a *joint memorial* in Yerevan *to the Holocaust and the Armenian Genocide* in October 2006.[*] Turkey in 2007 made an effort to send positive signals to the Armenians through its restoration of the famous Holy Cross Church at Aghtamar, on Lake Van. The gesture was not well received by all segments of the Armenian community, in part because there was no cross installed on top of the church, which has been converted to a museum, and because the place name was Turkicized to "Akdamar." The timing was also suspect: originally the church's re-opening was set precisely for April 24, the date on which, in 1915, the first Armenian intellectuals were rounded up, and the draping of enormous Turkish flags and portraits of Atatürk on the restored church did not help. These objections, it seems to me, are understandable, but ultimately, given the history of wholesale destruction of Armenian culture in Anatolia over decades, any effort to repair even some of the damage ought to be welcomed, even if Ankara's motivations are suspect. The Armenian historian Ara Sarafian apparently agreed, calling the restoration of Holy Cross Church an important "peace offering" from Turkey.[†] There has since (in 2011) been another historic Armenian church reopened in

---

[*] See the US Embassy website (*www.usa.am*) for details, including photographs of the monument, which may be the first of its kind anywhere in the world. It unfortunately has also now been defaced.

[†] As quoted by PanArmenian.net 09.04.2007.

Diyarbekir. The wholesale restoration and return to the Armenians of churches, monasteries and other properties of historic and cultural significance should be the ultimate goal here. In places where restoration is not feasible, perhaps historical markers or plaques could be erected, as is the practice in other countries, including the United States.

8. Another step would involve counseling individual Armenian-American families. The State Department maintains an Office of Holocaust Issues that has been quietly working for many years to help bring a measure of assistance and justice to Holocaust victims and their families, and to create an infrastructure to assure the Holocaust is remembered properly and accurately. The Office has helped facilitate negotiations to reach various agreements on the subject of Holocaust-era claims. Several class-action suits in the 1990s set the stage for negotiation of a settlement agreement with Swiss banks, and executive agreements with Germany, France and Austria that dealt with claims arising from Holocaust-era insurance policies, among other things. The State Department's Special Envoy for Holocaust Issues sits on a number of boards overseeing the implementation of these agreements. So far as I can see, there is nothing in the mandate of this office to prevent its helping Armenian-Americans process private claims with insurance companies or the Government of Turkey. Claims by some 1,900 Armenians of Ottoman origin having U.S. citizenship were theoretically arbitrated in 1934, but in such a way that individual claims were effectively ignored.[*] The Treaty of Amity and Commerce that Washington and Ankara signed on August 6, 1923, though never ratified, took no note of Armenians' grievances. Today, other more recent treaties might be invoked to block any U.S. assistance to victims' families in processing claims. In 2013 the U.S. Supreme Court invited the Solicitor General to detail the U.S. position on the issue of claims against insurance companies pursued by descendants of Genocide survivors in accordance with a California law that was struck down by the Ninth Circuit Court in

---

[*] Bloxham, op. cit., p. 204.

early 2012. The Court's decision effectively closed the door to direct claims against Turkey, but the State Department, in consultation with Armenian claimants, could still explore the issue with a view to seeing what might be done.

9. What is needed as a precondition to further action on behalf of the victims of the Genocide – and for future generations of Armenian and Turkish students – is a very tough challenge: an agreed statement of the history, the facts, and the proper characterization of what happened in 1915 and afterward. For that to emerge, there would need to be a joint commission of historians, adequately insulated against political pressures from either the Turkish or the Armenian states, or political circles close to them. This idea was floated by Prime Minister Erdoğan in 2005, but rejected by Yerevan as unnecessary, given that – in the confirmed view of the Armenians and the vast preponderance of serious scholars – there is no doubt as to the reality of the Genocide. Yerevan did not rule out the possibility of discussing historical issues, but did not want the question of the Genocide to be the only one on the table, as there are even more pressing issues involving establishing normal diplomatic relations and opening the border. In March, 2007, then-Foreign Minister Abdullah Gül embellished this offer by suggesting that third-country historians might take part in such a historical commission, thus making it multilateral: "I hereby extend an invitation to any third country, including the United States, to contribute to this [historical] commission by appointing scholars..."* It seems to me that this idea that has some merit, despite the ever-present risk that one side or the other might drag its feet or obstruct the reaching of reasonable and mutually acceptable conclusions. In this connection, the Turkish historian Halil Berktay has, in a private communication, said the following about Gül's offer: "...this editorial contains other elements which, if subsequent developments were to be in a good direction, would derive a better or more progressive meaning from that positive

---

* Abdullah Gul, "Politicizing the Armenian Tragedy," Op-Ed in The Washington *Times*, March 28, 2007.

development. Otherwise put, it contains certain elements which, with a flexible strategy, could be jumped upon."[*] Dr. Berktay, it should be noted, made a similar suggestion at the NATO-sponsored Rose-Roth seminar in Yerevan in 2005. Newly-elected Armenian President Serzh Sargsyan told an Armenian audience in Moscow in 2008 that "we do not mind" the idea of a historical commission, but that "the land border between our countries should be opened first."[†] Armenians, despite misgivings, should realize that a historical commission would provide some measure of domestic face-saving for the Turkish State, and not dismiss it out of hand.

Joint historical commissions are not easy to organize or to sustain, and they can become the target of intense political criticism, but they have helped to forge shared histories in such previous fraught cases as France and Germany and Germany and Poland. The implications for teaching in the schools, for settling claims, and for establishing more normal relations are potentially enormous, and, in my view, outweigh the risks for both sides. There is a school of thought that does not like "top-down" efforts to prescribe what history is and is not, but ultimately school textbooks do need to be written and approved, even in the age of Wikipedia. In the meantime, some useful discussion of the historical facts has been quietly going on under the auspices of the Workshop for Armenian/Turkish Scholarship, a group of several hundred scholars who communicate primarily via a website and listserv founded in 2000 by Professors Fatma Müge Göçek, Kevork Bardakjian and others at the University of Michigan and Ronald Suny of the University of Chicago (and administered by Prof. Göçek). Despite some detractors, inevitable moments of irrelevance, and occasional outbursts of invective, the Workshop has proven

---

* Electronic communication to the Armenian-Turkish Workshop dated March 30, 2007.

† Reported June 24, 2008 by PanARMENIAN.net and subsequently in *Aravot* and elsewhere.

valuable, not least to the Turks.[*] As Os Guinness has written, "...the best way forward is partly to go back, so that the remembered past is the key to a renewed future, and a usable past is a liberal force..."[†]

10. What can we, as individual American citizens, do about the Armenian Genocide? First of all, *we can give Armenian-Americans our respect, and honor their narrative.* The great out-pouring of commentary that appeared in American media in October 2007 on the advisability of the House's passing a non-binding resolution on the Armenian Genocide demonstrated not only a strong *Realpolitik* consensus, but also an unfortunate tendency on the part of some commentators to belittle Armenians as a group. The Washington *Post* ran an editorial entitled, "Worse than Irrelevant."[‡] Other commentators called Speaker Pelosi's support of the measure "political pandering" and incorrectly suggested that her San Francisco district was the heart of the Armenian *diaspora* (it is actually Los Angeles). Still others referred to the Armenians' quest for recognition of the Genocide as a bit of "mischief," and a few suggested Armenian-Americans were "unpatriotic." Given the large number of Armenian-Americans who have worn the uniform of the United States in World War II, Korea, Vietnam and other conflicts, this accusation sits very badly with Armenian-Americans.[**] While it was not difficult to argue, in terms of U.S. interests, that the timing of H. Res. 106, "Affirmation of the United States Record on the Armenian Genocide" was poor, what was sad to witness was the tone of disrespect for Armenians that all too frequently accompanied the

---

[*] The website is *www.armturkworkshop.org.* WATS won the MESA Academic Freedom Prize in 2005.

[†] Os. Guiness, *The Case for Civility: And Why Our Future Depends on It.* (New York: Harper Collins, 2008), p. 81.

[‡] The Washington *Post*, October 10, 2007.

[**] Anyone doubting the contributions Armenian-Americans have made to this country's defense should have a look at *The Faces of Courage: Armenian World War II, Korea and Vietnam Heroes*, by Richard Demirjian (Moraga, CA: Ararat Heritage Publishing, 2003).

logical, prudential arguments. So *the most important thing we all can do is not to disrespect the Armenians.* They are the bearers of an ancient culture that far antedates our own. They have been the victims of history, were traumatized by the genocide, and yet have contributed richly to the countries, most notably the United States, to which they made their way after "the Great Catastrophe." Their quest for affirmation of the Genocide is no surprise and no crime. Stating a historical fact cannot in itself be considered offensive or insolent, although there are clearly more and less aggressive ways of going about it, and the firm, but polite and respectful, approach usually works best, though it requires patience.

My advice to American diplomats and others who want to avoid disrespecting their Armenian-American fellow citizens is to avoid any of the following actions – really techniques of denial – with regard to the Armenian Genocide: 1) negating it outright; 2) casting doubt on whether it happened; 3) engaging in debate as to whether it happened; 4) rationalizing it; 5) relativizing it; or 6) trivializing it.[*] This is not a call for censorship or for not discussing the matter at all. I do not agree with those parliaments that have made denial of the Armenian Genocide a crime punishable by law. But for too long we have tolerated, in some cases even contributed to, unseemly disregard of both the facts of history (if not outright denial) and of the understandable feelings of the Armenians. To put it positively, learning about the facts of history is a way of countering the policy of official denial, and treating the subject with the sensitivity it deserves is a way of ministering to the great psychic wounds that remain. As a political matter, we would do well also to be mindful of how difficult coming to terms with their own history is going to be for the Turks, while pressing them to do so. Heirs to a complicated and difficult

---

[*] Richard Hovannisian mentions four of these six strategies of denial in his essay "Denial of the Armenian Genocide in Comparison with Holocaust Denial" in Hovannisian, Richard G., ed., *Remembrance and Denial: The Case of the Armenian Genocide.* Detroit: Wayne State University Press, 1999, p. 201.

legacy, today's Turks deserve to be treated with dignity and respect, so long as they have the courage and decency to acknowledge the misdeeds of the past. If the Armenians among us see that their own story is honored and respected in this country, they are more likely to feel truly comfortable here and to "assimilate" in the best sense of that word: not losing their special identity, but even more decisively joining the American mainstream.

Beyond not "disrespecting" the Armenians, and honoring their narrative, we all need to take more interest in the current challenge of stopping genocide in the world. We can write to the news media and our elected representatives in support of better education on the subject of genocide – past and present – with an aim to prevent this crime from happening again and going unpunished in the future. The combined efforts of Armenian, Jewish and Irish groups, as well as the NAACP, in Massachusetts resulted in a court decision there to permit the Massachusetts public schools to provide genocide education – including the Armenian Genocide – and to prohibit competing "denialist" narratives from having equal billing.[*]

Historical events in themselves cannot be changed, although their interpretation can be, and constantly is, by ever-younger generations of historians with fresh approaches and sometimes new tools of research. In dealing with the Armenian Genocide – and its consequences – both our memories of the past and our hopes for the future need to be invoked. Much energy has been expended on elucidating the past; we now know as much, perhaps, as we need to know about the events, although there are always new pieces of the picture turning up. The tragedy and the horror of it all need to be memorialized, in part as insurance against its repetition, and also as a compensation, partly psychological, hopefully also tangible, to the victims and their survivors. There must also be attention paid to the future, that is, to the children of the survivors, the children of Armenia. There is one organization, private and non-political, which

---

[*] June 10, 2009 decision of U.S. District Court Chief Judge Mark Wolf in *Griswold v. Driscoll.*

is doing exactly that: the Children of Armenia Fund. Based in New York, this organization (known as COAF) has been quietly, with little fanfare, reconstructing villages in southwestern Armenia, not just physical elements like schools and community centers, but the very health, education and lives of village children there, many if not most of whom are descendants of Armenians who fled the ravages of the Genocide. For those who wish to contribute to the future health of the Armenian people, COAF and other organizations like it are doing important, even vital, work to repair the damaged fabric of the nation, and need support.

Similarly, there is a worthy project underway at the University of Southern California. The Shoah Foundation, which Steven Spielberg set up in 1994 after the success of his film *Schindler's List,* has been based at USC since 2006, and has collected some 52,000 eyewitness accounts of the Holocaust. In the meantime, the Armenian film-maker Michael Hagopian, founder of the Armenian Film Foundation, had been assiduously collecting and filming the oral testimonies of survivors of the Armenian Genocide. In 2010, Dr. Hagopian and his wife, Antoinette, reached an agreement with what is now the USC Shoah Foundation to license the 400 survivor testimonies and make them available in digital form to its Visual History Archive. This work is underway, and will eventually make it possible for students and others around the world to access these valuable materials. The effort is, however, costly, and needs resources, at last count, about $900,000, to reach completion.

There is so much that needs to be done that any and all efforts are precious.

Thinking Ahead

Genocide is perhaps the most awful of crimes, adding up to more than the sum of all the murders and other crimes that together comprise it. Thus it is no surprise that the young Soghomon Tehlirian, whose family was wiped out in the Armenian Genocide, took justice into his own hands and assassinated Talaat Pasha in

Berlin in 1921. In that case, the German court, understanding Tehlirian's personal pain, acquitted him for the murder of Talaat, who, in any case, had been sentenced *in absentia* to death by an Ottoman court-martial.* It also was not a complete surprise that in the 1970s and 1980s the Armenian Secret Army for the Liberation of Armenia (ASALA) carried out a vicious campaign of assassination against Turkish diplomats and their families, none of whom could personally be considered guilty of any crime. That period fortunately ended years ago, although Turkish diplomatic families known to me and some of my Foreign Service colleagues still feel the pain of their losses. Taking justice into one's own hands is fraught with many dangers and philosophical questions, but it is a natural human reaction when a crime has been committed for which there has been no retribution or punishment – or even acknowledgement. The world has rightly become altogether less tolerant of terrorism in the service of whatever cause.

The pursuit of parliamentary and Congressional resolutions affirming the fact of the Armenian Genocide may strike some of us "un-hyphenated" Americans as strange, extreme, or even obsessive. We have not seen it as our history or our struggle; rather we have viewed it as something exotic from another – and benighted – part of the world. The struggle of African-Americans for their civil rights and dignity was not seen by many white Americans as their cause either, yet many white people eventually joined or supported the civil rights movement, some by going to Selma to march, others by contributing to the NAACP or (like my father) the United Negro College Fund. If the emancipated slaves, as promised, had received their "forty acres and a mule" after the Civil War, the inequities and struggles of the following century might have been very different. Similarly, if the promises made to the Armenians after World War I had been

---

* Power, op. cit., pp. 1-16, tells the story well. For a fuller account, see *The Case of Soghomon Tehlirian*, by Vartkes Yeghiayan .(Glendale, California; Center for Armenian Remembrance, 2006)

respected, the Armenians might not today be seeking a substitute for justice in the form of parliamentary resolutions.

And yet, today's world cannot live by the rule of "a tooth for a tooth." As Gandhi observed, "when the law 'an eye for an eye' is applied, everyone ends up blind."

There are others ways forward, but none of them is easy.

During the 1960s a remarkable thing happened in the relations between Poland and the Federal Republic of Germany. In November 1965, Polish Catholic Bishops wrote a "Letter of Reconciliation" to their German counterparts, saying "we forgive and ask forgiveness," even though the crimes against Poland committed by Germany during the Second World War were surely far greater than the reverse. Archbishop Karol Wojtyla – the future Pope John Paul – supported the Letter, which infuriated the Communist authorities of the time. Eventually, as we saw, Chancellor Willy Brandt knelt before the Warsaw Ghetto, other acts of expiation were undertaken by the Germans, and relations between the two countries were set on an entirely new course. It was not an easy process. Historical commissions labored for years to construct a new, objective narrative of German-Polish relations, and new school text-books were published for use in both countries. Now the two former enemies are both in the European Union and, although strains occasionally surface, their common border is a peaceful one. The Letter of the Polish Bishops stands as a remarkable example of Christian teaching at work: how "undeserved kindness awakens the remorse and hence conversion of the enemies."[*]

At some point in the future, even if it turns out to be the far distant future, would it be in character for Armenians, the world's first Christian nation, to *forgive* the Turks for what (some of) their ancestors did in 1915? It would not be easy to do this, and *it could not*

---

[*] Editors of the *New Oxford Annotated Bible*, as quoted by Robert Wright, New York *Times*, April 7, 2007, p. A13. Wright rightly cautions that "Sometimes it does, sometimes it doesn't."

be done without sincere, far-reaching, public remorse on the part of the Republic of Turkey, including some effort on Ankara's part to make at least partial amends. The situation that faced the Poles and the Germans is not comparable to that which exists between the Armenians and the Turks: there is no Turkish Episcopate for the Armenian bishops to address, and – most importantly of all, Turkey has not taken the courageous steps of admission and contrition that Germany has taken. At present it is difficult to imagine that such a sequence of truth-telling, apology and forgiving could ever happen, so fraught are the relations between the Turks and their neighbors – and Armenian Diasporans; however, one day it might start. There is great power in the act of forgiving, and it should not be done lightly, but it is the final ingredient of the healing that is ultimately necessary. Former Archbishop Desmond Tutu, a true pioneer in the area of truth and reconciliation, has wisely spoken of the power that resides in the act of forgiving, and of the "ultimate grace of forgiveness." Addressing a crowd on the Centennial of the Washington Cathedral, Tutu said, "Forgiveness is not a sentimental, namby-pamby thing. It is costly. It cost God the death of God's Son. It is not for sissies. It has nothing in common with the facile expression, 'forgive and forget.' No, forgiveness stares the beast in the eye, is confrontational. To name the hurt, the cause of the upset, and to refuse to retaliate: it is not retributive but restorative; it seeks not to punish but to heal. We remember so that we in our turn may not inflict the same wrong on another."[*]

The Canadian philosopher and spiritual teacher Eckhart Tolle, in his book *A New Earth*, describes how the pain of the past lives on in individuals and in groups or even nations. He calls this "accumulation of old emotional pain" the "pain-body."[†] He describes how the pain-body renews itself through thoughts, emotions and

---

[*] At the Washington National Cathedral, November 13, 2007.

[†] Eckhart Tolle, *A New Earth: Awakening to Your Life's Purpose.* (New York: Dutton, 2005), p. 140.

dramas, and notes that "older nations tend to have stronger pain-bodies," whereas younger countries have lighter ones. Though he does not mention the Armenians, Tolle writes that the "collective racial pain-body is pronounced in Jewish people, who have suffered persecution over many centuries." He also sees it as being strong among Native Americans and African-Americans. Proposing a solution, Tolle advises, "Even if blame seems more than justified, as long as you blame others, you keep feeding the pain-body with your thoughts and remain trapped in your ego. There is only one perpetrator of evil on the planet: human unconsciousness. That realization is true forgiveness."[*]

While I leave it entirely to individual Armenians themselves to ponder whether Tolle's prescription works to any degree for them, I suggest simply that both Turks and Armenians think about the two tools available to them – apology and forgiving – as "unthinkable" as wielding them might seem to both parties. Even if neither side can bring itself to apologize or to forgive, or even to agree on the truth of the matter, the right approach is what Os Guinness has called for in *The Case for Civility*, in which he wrestles with the reality that we all must live despite our "deep differences." Guinness writes, "[w]hat we are looking for is not so much truths that can unite us as terms on which we can negotiate and by which we can live with the differences that divide us."[†]

All of us, Armenians, Turks and Americans (who want to be good friends to both) need to think about what we, individually and collectively, can do to hasten the day of *both truth __and__ reconciliation*, but in the meantime to do what is possible given continuing disagreement and differences. Seemingly small efforts, such as the concert that Turkish and Armenian student groups endeavored, unsuccessfully, to organize at Brown University in April 2007, on the theme of Armenian Composers in the Ottoman Empire, ought to be

---

* Ibid., pp. 159-60.

† Guinness, op. cit., p. 149.

encouraged rather than torpedoed. Larger cultural exchange efforts like the reciprocal performances of the Bosporus and the Komitas Quartets that took place in June 2008 under the auspices of the Eurasia Partnership Foundation also aim at instilling mutual respect and fostering reconciliation. When the President of Armenia invited the Turkish President to Yerevan to watch their respective football teams play in the World Cup competition, this Caucasian twist on "ping-pong diplomacy" was rightly applauded. Ultimately, Armenians and Turks are destined to live side by side in Asia Minor and the Caucasus, and their far-flung fellow-countrymen also will be living together in German, French, Russian, Canadian and American cities. Hatred and mutually destructive vendettas must eventually be replaced, even if gradually, by mutual tolerance and respect, but this must be based on an honest acceptance of past history, not its denial.

But what about grief, and grieving? There are fewer than one hundred survivors of the Armenian Genocide still with us on the centenary of that event. The Roman stoic philosopher Seneca the Younger recalled, in a letter to his mother, that

> …our ancestors allowed widows to mourn their husbands for ten months, in order to compromise by public decree with the stubbornness of female grief. They did not prohibit mourning, but they limited it. For to be afflicted with endless sorrow at the loss of someone very dear is foolish self-indulgence, and to feel none is inhuman callousness.[*]

The continuing talks on settling the dispute between Armenia and Azerbaijan over Nagorno-Karabakh, in which Russia, France and the United States have served as mediators, are extremely important; indeed, they are crucial to a better future for all the peoples of the South Caucasus. Although the Genocide is not a direct issue in the Nagorno-Karabakh dispute, its long shadow and the shadows of other, more recent, atrocities hang over the proceedings. Notably, the

[*] Seneca the Younger, "Consolation to Helvia," in *Dialogues and Letters*, Penguin Classics, 1997, reprinted as *On the Shortness of Life*; London, Penguin Books, 2004, p. 59.

2003 axe-murder of a sleeping Armenian officer by an Azerbaijani officer while both were attending a NATO-sponsored training session in Budapest, and the hero's welcome given to the Azeribaijani, Ramil Safarov, in 2012, when he was released from prison custody in Hungary and sent back to Baku, could reasonably be considered genocidal. While the situation in the South Caucasus cannot today be considered pre-genocidal, lives are being lost every year along the Line of Contact to sniper fire from both sides. Both sides should pull back their snipers, as the OSCE has recommended.[*] Were the outright hostilities of the early 1990s ever to resume in a major way, as some Azerbaijani politicians and officials have threatened, there could indeed be serious consequences for both sides, although the basic facts on the ground are unlikely to be altered at this point by military or diplomatic action. What is needed is skillful diplomacy backed up by high-level attention in the relevant capitals. Eventually, it will be necessary for the international community to assist the Armenians and the Azerbaijanis to rebuild the areas damaged during the Karabakh conflict.

For all their present differences and past conflicts, Turks and Armenians share a glorious, if sometimes bloody, history and many elements of culture. The Armenians contributed heavily to the richness of Ottoman life. And the Ottomans, for much of their long ascendancy, were not the worst imaginable rulers, at least by the standards of their day, even though their empire was hardly a model of fairness, and non-Muslims like the Armenians constituted, in many respects, second-class subjects. For that matter, Armenians and Azerbaijanis share a long history of friendship and commerce in the Russian Empire and the Soviet Union (as well as in Iran). What I think the leaders of both communities need to do now is to back away from the most extreme nationalistic rhetoric and claims, the most exaggerated national stereotypes, and edge back toward the tolerant and reasonable middle, where both sides can prosper in the

---

[*] At the December 2008 OSCE Ministerial Meeting in Helsinki. Armenia has agreed to the recommendation; Azerbaijan has not.

future. Squarely facing the facts of shared history is a condition *sine qua non* for doing so. The religious leaders on both sides can help. The United States ought not to stand in the way by embracing a policy that is essentially a formula for permanent denial and deadlock. The title of an article on this subject by Samantha Power sums it up: "Honesty is the Best Policy. Recognizing the Armenian Genocide may seem risky, but keeping quiet is the bigger danger."[*]

Truth matters. History matters. And justice also matters. But as we seek the truth, affirm the true facts of history, and struggle to mitigate the effects of past injustices, we need urgently also to build a world where genocide can truly never happen again. Too often it seems that the vow "never again!" has meant only that "never again would Germans kill Jews in Europe in the 1940s,"[†] while actual genocides – in Cambodia, in Rwanda, in Darfur – have continued to occur and have been tolerated. This is not to detract from the significance of the Holocaust, which remains in a category all its own. The lessons of the Armenian Genocide – which teach with special force the corrosive consequences of denial – must be taught, learned and incorporated into our political culture, just as the lessons of the Holocaust have been. America and Americans must stand firmly on the solid high ground of truth and honesty, while showing by our own example how to face history.

Afterword

My own voyage of discovery of the Armenians and of the truth about the Armenian Genocide has now effectively ended, bringing me full circle, back to America and to some newly troubling thoughts closer to home. For when we start looking into these difficult issues like genocide, the search may lead us anywhere.

In the Virginia public schools, we learned a certain version of our state's history. We learned about the English settlers, who established

---

[*] *TIME,* October 29, 2007.

[†] The observation is originally David Rieff's.

at Jamestown the first permanent English-speaking colony in the New World. It was and remains a glorious story, even though it largely ignored ten thousand years of indigenous Native American civilization and glossed over the hideous realities of slavery. What I now see more clearly than ever before, with perspective gained from time, distance and from my study of the Armenian Genocide, is that my own home state of Virginia and our Federal government, for that matter, were far from guiltless on at least two major counts: the campaigns we waged – at times genocidal in nature – against the original natives of this continent, and the brutalities of slavery, including its latter-day – and arguably genocidal – phenomenon, lynching. General Sheridan's dictum, "The only good Indian is a dead Indian" is, on the face of it, a genocidal statement. The Trail of Tears of the Cherokee and the Long March of the Navajo were arguably genocidal chapters in our own history. The new Museum of the American Indian on the National Mall now stands in belated recognition of the destruction of America's first inhabitants but also, happily, of their contributions to our modern life and of their tenacity and will to survive. The future Museum of African-American History on the Mall will do something similar for African-Americans.

In recent years, the prime ministers of Australia and Canada have issued public apologies for past treatment of aboriginal and native Indian populations, in particular the practice of attempting forcibly to assimilate native children through boarding schools that had as their goal to "wash out" their previous identity. This news brought me up with a start: my own father, for a time, occupied an office at the College of William and Mary in the former Brafferton Indian School, where Indian boys were prepared for the Anglican priesthood. I have recently learned that some of my own Pennsylvania ancestors had African-American servants, possibly slaves, and that one distant cousin, John Evans, the second governor of the Colorado Territory, a friend of Lincoln's and a co-founder of the Illinois Republican Party, was deemed responsible for ordering the Sand Creek massacre of Cheyenne and Arapaho Indians in 1864

Mt. Evans in Colorado.

– and for attempting to cover it up. He was removed from office; nevertheless, Mt. Evans in Colorado (at 14,265 feet, a "fourteener") is still named for him.

Are we Americans, then, any different from the Turks (or other nations) in willfully forgetting, if not actively denying, the sins of our ancestors? I am not the one to answer that question. I can only suggest that democracy and free speech, in a "civil public square" are the proper antidotes to denial and suppression of historical facts. Neither American democracy nor democracy as practiced in Turkey or Armenia or Azerbaijan is perfect. Neither we Virginia schoolchildren nor the vast majority of Turkish or Armenian children were adequately informed about the realities of the past. No doubt the past was selectively recalled in the service of our own patriotic instincts and put in the service of our national myths. This was not unusual or unique or perhaps even wrong for its time. But it is now time to learn of these things, to show moral leadership, to apologize for crimes and excesses, to make what amends can still be made after the passage of time, and, yes, also to forgive, without, however, forgetting.

Acknowledging past mistakes should be seen as an act of affirmation, not of self-humiliation. We must all of us – each nation – forge a new kind of national unity, self-critical, reflective, wise and humble, in each of our countries, incorporating the full truth about our bloody and yet stirring pasts while creating a new spirit of understanding, tolerance and respect for all, in the emerging "global public square."[*]

On April 12, 2015, Pope Francis spoke eloquently of the Armenian Genocide during an Armenian-rite Mass in St. Peter's Basilica in Rome. He mentioned also that Christians of the Middle East (and, he might also have mentioned, other minorities such as the Yazidis) are still falling victim to the genocidal impulse that humanity has not tamed. The Turkish Government reacted heatedly and recalled its Ambassador. We have a long way to go before we can even agree on what has happened in the past.

Looking further ahead, far beyond the scope of this book, I believe the world ultimately needs to find practical ways to transcend, or at least to contain, the narrow ethnic nationalism and religious tribalism that has been responsible for so much human suffering, and to embrace decisively a broader concept of a shared humanity. Short of a threat emanating from Mars or another galaxy, the odds are clearly against our doing so anytime soon, but in the long run the future of our imperiled planet demands it. And the United States, because it is a "nation of nations," and uniquely blessed, remains, despite all its warts and failings, the "last, best hope of Earth."

---

[*] Os Guinness's phrase.

Bibliography

Aftandilian, Gregory L., *Armenia, Vision of a Republic: The Independence Lobby in America 1918-1927,* Charlestown MA: Charles River Books, 1981.

Akçam, Taner, *From Empire to Republic: Turkish Nationalism & the Armenian Genocide,* London: Zed Books, 2004.

Akçam, Taner, *A Shameful Act: The Armenian Genocide and the Question of Turkish Responsibility,* New York: Metropolitan Books, 2006.

Akçam, Taner, *The Young Turks' Crime Against Humanity,* Princeton: Princeton University Press, 2012.

Balakian, Grigoris, *Armenian Golgotha: A Memoir of the Armenian Genocide, 1915-1918,* translated by Peter Balakian with Aris Sevag, New York: Knopf, 2009.

Balakian, Peter, *Black Dog of Fate: A Memoir,* New York: Broadway Books, 1997.

Balakian, Peter, *The Burning Tigris: The Armenian Genocide and America's Response,* New York: HarperCollins, 2003.

Barton, James L. *"Turkish Atrocities": Statements of American Missionaries on the Destruction of Christian Communities in Ottoman Turkey, 1915-1917,* Ann Arbor MI: Gomidas Institute, 1998.

Bazyler, Michael J., ed., *Raphael Lemkin's Dossier on the Armenian Genocide,* Glendale CA: Center for Armenian Remembrance, 2008.

Bloxham, Donald, *The Great Game of Genocide: Imperialism, Nationalism, and the Destruction of the Ottoman Armenians,* New York: Oxford University Press, 2005.

Bobelian, Michael, *Children of Armenia: A Forgotten Genocide and the Century-Long Struggle for Justice,* New York: Simon & Schuster, 2009.

Dadrian, Vahakn N., and Akçam, Taner, *Judgment at Istanbul: The Armenian Genocide Trials,* New York: Berghahn Books, 2011 (Turkish-language edition 2008).

Dadrian, Vahakn N., *German Responsibility in the Armenian Genocide: A Review of the Historical Evidence of German Complicity,* Cambridge MA: Blue Crane Books, 1996.

Dadrian, Vahakn N., *The Ottoman Empire: A Troubled Legacy*, Yerevan: International Association of Genocide Scholars, 2010.

Davis, Leslie A., *The Slaughterhouse Province: An American Diplomat's Report on the Armenian Genocide, 1915-1917*, New Rochelle NY: Aristide D. Caratzas, 1989.

De Bellaigue, Christopher, *Rebel Land: Unraveling the Riddle of History in a Turkish Town*, New York: Penguin, 2010.

Demirjian, Richard N., *Triumph and Glory: Armenian World War II Heroes*, Moraga CA: Ararat Heritage Publishing, 1996.

De Waal, Thomas, *Black Garden: Armenia and Azerbaijan through Peace and War*, New York: New York University Press, 2003.

De Waal, Thomas, *The Caucasus: An Introduction*, Oxford University Press.

De Zayas, Alfred, *The Genocide Against the Armenians, 1915-1923, and the Relevance of the 1948 Genocide Convention*, Beirut: Haigazian University Press, 2010.

Fromkin, David, *A Peace to End All Peace: The Fall of the Ottoman Empire and the Creation of the Modern Middle East*, New York: Henry Holt, 1989.

Gregorian, Vartan, *The Road to Home: My Life and Times*, New York: Simon & Schuster, 2004.

Guiness, Os, *The Case for Civility and Why Our Future Depends on It*, New York: Harper Collins, 2008.

New York: Hovannisian, Richard G., ed., *The Armenian People from Ancient to Modern Times*, 2 vols. New York: St. Martin's Press, 1997.

Hovannisian, Richard G., ed., *Remembrance and Denial: The Case of the Armenian Genocide*, Detroit: Wayne State University Press, 1999.

Hovannisian, Richard G., ed., *Looking Backward, Moving Forward: Confronting the Armenian Genocide*, New Brunswick NJ: Transaction Publishers, 2003.

Hovannisian, Richard G., ed., *The Armenian Genocide in Perspective*, New Brunswick, NJ: Transaction Publishers, 2003.

Hovannisian, Richard G., ed., *The Armenian Genocide: Cultural and Ethical Legacies*, New Brunswick, NJ: Transaction Publishers, 2008.

Hovhannisyan, Nikolay, *The Armenian Genocide: Armenocide: Causes, Commission Consequences*, Yerevan, Institute of Oriental Studies of the National Academy of Armenia.

Jerjian, George, *The Truth Will Set Us Free*, London: GJ Communications, 2002.

Kinross, Baron John P. D. B., *The Ottoman Centuries: the Rise and Fall of the Turkish Empire*, New York: Morrow, 1977.

Kirakossian, Arman J., British *Diplomacy and the Armenian Question from the 1830s to 1914*, Princeton: Gomidas Institute, 2003.

Kirakossian, Arman J., ed., *The Armenian Massacres, 1894-1896: U.S. Media Testimony*, Detroit: Wayne State University Press, 2004.

Kloian, Richard D., *The Armenian Genocide: News Accounts from the American Press*, Richmond, CA: ACC Books, 1980.

Lewy, Guenter, *The Armenian Massacres in Ottoman Turkey: A Disputed Genocide*, Salt Lake City: University of Utah Press, 2005.

Libaridian, Gerard J., *Modern Armenia: People, Nation, State*, New Brunswick NJ: Transaction Publishers, 2004.

Lind, Jennifer, *Sorry States: Apologies in International Politics*, Ithaca: Cornell University Press, 2008.

McCarthy, Justin, et. al., *The Armenian Rebellion at Van*, Salt Lake City: University of Utah Press, 2006.

McMeekin, Sean, *The Russian Origins of the First World War*, Belknap Press, 2011

Morgenthau, Henry, *Ambassador Morgenthau's Story*, New York: Doubleday, 1918.

Panossian, Razmik, *The Armenians: From Kings and Priests to Merchants and Commissars*, New York: Columbia University Press, 2006.

Papian, Ara, ed., *Arbitral Award of the President of the United States of America Woodrow Wilson: Full Report of the Committee Upon the Arbitration of the Boundary Between Turkey and Armenia*, Issued November 22, 1920 and republished with an introduction, notes and indices on the basis of National Archives microfilm. Yerevan: "Asoghik" Publishing House, 2011.

Payaslian, Simon, *The History of Armenia: From the Origins to the Present*, New York: Palgrave Macmillan, 2007.

Phillips, David L., *Unsilencing the Past: Track Two Diplomacy and Turkish-Armenian Reconciliation*, New York: Berghahn Books, 2005.

Phillips, David L., *Diplomatic History: The Turkey-Armenia Protocols*, New York: Columbia Institute for the Study of Human Rights, 2012.

Power, Samantha, *"A Problem From Hell": America and the Age of Genocide*, New York: Basic Books, 2003.

Sarafian, Ara, ed. *United States Official Records on the Armenian Genocide,* London and Princeton: Gomidas Institute, 2004.

Sassounian, Harut, *The Armenian Genocide: The World Speaks Out, 1915-2005: Documents and Declarations,* Glendale CA: 90th Anniversary of the Armenian Genocide Commemorative Committee of California, 2005.

Shaw, Stanford and Ezel Kural Shaw, *History of the Ottoman Empire and Modern Turkey, vol. II, Reform, Revolution and Republic: The Rise of Modern Turkey,* Cambridge: Cambridge University Press, 1977.

Sontag, Susan, *Regarding the Pain of Others,* New York: Picador, 2003.

Suny, Ronald Grigor, Fatma Müge Göçek and Norman M. Naimark, editors, *A Question of Genocide: Armenians and Turks at the End of the Ottoman Empire,* Oxford University Press, 2011.

Svazlian, Verjiné, *The Armenian Genocide and the People's Historical Memory,* Yerevan: Gitutiun, 2005.

Tolle, Eckhart, *A New Earth: Awakening to Life's Purpose,* New York: Dutton, 2005.

Totten, Samuel, William D. Parsons and Israel W. Charny, eds., *Century of Genocide: Critical Essays and Eyewitness Accounts,* New York: Routledge, 2004.

Ussher, Clarence D., *An American Physician in Turkey: A Narrative of Adventures in Peace and War,* Boston: Houghton Mifflin, 1917, Facsimile edition: Woodside NY: J. C. and A. L. Fawcett, 1990.

Yeghiayan, Vartkes, *The Case of Soghomon Tehlirian,* Glendale CA: Center for Armenian Remembrance, 2006.

Yeghiayan, Vartkes, ed. *British Reports on Ethnic Cleansing in Anatolia, 1919-1922: The Armenian-Greek Section.* Glendale CA: Center for Armenian Remembrance, 2007.

Winter, Jay, ed. *America and the Armenian Genocide of 1915.* Cambridge: Cambridge University Press, 2003.

INDEX